Praise for *Unschooling in Paradise*

Kathleen Kesson is a poet—a lyrical, beckoning and righteously angry poet…(she) is uncommonly generous in her willingness to so vividly share the magnificent stories of her children learning the world.

— Sheri Leafgren, Ph.D., Associate Professor of Teacher Education, Miami University, author of *Reuben's Fall: A Rhizomatic Analysis of Disobedience in Kindergarten*

Unschooling in Paradise gets to the heart of teaching and learning because for Kathleen young people are flesh and blood minds, bodies, and spirits set in the context of their time, not some researcher's construct. And she tells one mean story along the way.

— Chris Mercogliano, author of *Making It Up as We Go Along and In Defense of Childhood: Protecting Kids' Inner Wildness*

…the descriptions about how her children learned through their own curiosity and play will encourage homeschoolers, and her knowledge of education theory and practice will help those who are on the fence about trusting their children's self-directed learning

— Patrick Farenga, president and publisher, John Holt Growing Without Schooling

…a masterful memoir-manifesto that takes the baton from the great thinkers in and on education—including John Dewey, John Holt, Ivan Illich—and races forward. Her masterpiece reads as a "love letter" of sorts, one that could not have come at a more needed time.

— Dana L. Stuchul, Ph.D., Associate Professor, Penn State University, co-author of *Teaching as if Life Matters: The Promise of a New Education Culture.*

Every page of this book is written to celebrate the fact that genius is as common as dirt -- once we begin to walk on our own feet on soil with common sense for regenerating our cultural commons.

— Madhu S. Prakash, Ph.D., Professor Emeritus of Education, Penn State University, author, *Grassroots Post-Modernism: Remaking the Soil of Cultures* and *Escaping Education: Living as Learning at the Grassroots*

This remarkable family experiment with unschooling illuminates the role of creativity and joy in children's education, and the depth and breadth of knowledge and experiences available to children in alternative learning contexts.

— Kellie Rolstad, Ph.D., Associate Professor of Applied Linguistics and Language Education, University of Maryland.

Kathleen brings together in these pages a deep wisdom for an integrated and nurturing form of education that is eminently doable. Read this book, share it with friends and put its insights into practice!

— Marcus Bussey, Ph.D., Senior Lecturer in History and Futures Studies, University of the Sunshine Coast, author, *Alternative Educational Futures*.

In this captivating and informative narrative, Kesson answers many questions that those contemplating or practicing unschooling often have...a rich and helpful book.

— Carlo Ricci, Ph.D., Professor, Schulich School of Education, Nipissing University, author of *The Willed Curriculum, Unschooling, and Self-Direction: What Do Love, Trust, Respect, Care, and Compassion Have To Do With Learning?* and founding editor, *Journal of Unschooling* and *Alternative Learning*.

UNSCHOOLING IN PARADISE

UNSCHOOLING IN PARADISE

KATHLEEN KESSON

InnerWorld Publications
San Germán, Puerto Rico
www.innerworldpublications.com

Published in the United States by InnerWorld Publications, P.O. Box 1613, San Germán, Puerto Rico, 00683

Library of Congress Control Number: 2018905140

ISBN: 9781881717621

Layout and Cover Design © Devashish Donald Acosta

Cover photo © Kel Pickens

To Steven, Shaman, Räm, and Chris
I love you all fiercely

and your wonderful wives and daughters: Kine, Ayesha, Alexa,
Revati, Anika, and Freya

and to Earl
who still dreams of a world without fences

A thousand gifts were given to us in the womb.
We lost hundreds during the forgetfulness of birth,
And we lost the old heaven on the first day of school.

~Robert Bly

Cease conceiving of education as mere preparation for later
life, and make it the full meaning of the present life.

~John Dewey

Contents

Preface
Do We Need School?

THE QUESTION IS NOT "Do we need education?" or "Do we need learning?" New people are always being born—right now, at the rate of about nine thousand an hour, despite the ardent efforts of the Voluntary Human Extinction movement, which promotes the idea that we must cease to breed in order to save the planet. We humans are hardwired to pass on what we have learned and gleaned through hard experience to our offspring. Even when they aren't terribly interested, which tends to be much of the time, especially when they turn fourteen. But do we need *school* to do that?

School as we know it is a relatively recent invention. *Compulsory* schooling is even more recent, dating in the US from the 1840's. Young people have always learned from their elders, but they learned practical skills, appropriate behavior, and moral wisdom largely through working alongside grown-ups and listening to stories told around the campfire or hearth. Book learning was fairly specialized in the past—the province of monks and aristocrats with a lot of time on their hands—and since books were expensive, nonlocalized knowledge that didn't relate to crop cycles and animal husbandry, like Latin verbs and world geography, was scarce. If you wanted to learn that stuff, you needed school, or at least a print-literate tutor.

Modern schooling is a form of social organization in which large numbers of young people are gathered together in a building, separated by age, under the supervision and tutelage of a much smaller number of professional adults who to varying degrees have expertise in some combination of "subject matter" and the arts of teaching. These pedagogical arts include such things as how to get a large group of kids all focused on one task that they may care little about, how to mediate conflicts and prevent chairs from being thrown, and increasingly, how to fill out vast amounts of paperwork documenting everything from behavioral incidents to whether a given child has met their IEP goals for the week. And unfortunately, the administrivia inherent in the job prevents most teachers from doing the one thing that both common sense and research tells us contributes to student learning, which is developing strong, authentic relationships with kids. Thus the discomforting question: "What is the *purpose* of schools?

Schools serve social functions much larger than student learning. The American public school movement really picked up steam in the midnineteenth century when some well intentioned radicals like Mother Jones decided that it wasn't such a good idea for children as young as ten to be working in dangerous factories where they didn't see the sunlight for twelve hours a day and were likely to get a finger or two chopped off. But we couldn't just have all those scruffy, illiterate kids running around the streets stealing apples all day. We needed some mechanism that could control the unruly young immigrants. We needed to *Americanize* them. Teach them the Protestant/Puritan values of the dominant WASP class and train them in the necessary skills for modern, urban, industrial culture: obedience, punctuality, docility, and the willingness to engage in mindless, repetitive labor for long periods of time in exchange for a meager wage.

To accomplish this, schools would need to be designed in particular ways. No walking in the woods with Socratic intellectuals who might pose questions intended to awaken intellectual curiosity, cause one to question authority, or challenge prevailing wisdom. No, we would need hard chairs set up in rows to control boisterous bodies, and prescribed periods of learning punctuated by ear-shattering bells just like the ones that summoned folks to work and marked the end of shifts in factories. Proper behavior would be reinforced with such pedagogical accessories as cane switches and dunce caps. Most importantly, knowledge would be dispensed in prescribed doses by authority figures and everyone would learn the same thing at the same time, all the better to ensure social stability through a common curriculum.

Unlike the present time, when we employ euphemisms like "individual achievement" and "critical thinking" and "equal opportunity" to mask the fact that school is really designed to produce a highly stratified labor force for the global economy, back at the beginning of the public school movement, elite school managers and policy makers were disturbingly straightforward about the need to train a work force for the emerging modern industrial economy. Here's a telling quote from a famous school superintendent, Ellwood Cubberly, at the dawn of the twentieth century:

> Our schools are in a sense, factories in which the raw materials are to be shaped and fashioned into products to meet the various demands of life. The specifications for manufacturing come from the demands of the twentieth century civilization, and it is the business of the school to build its pupils to the specifications laid down. This demands good tools, specialized machinery, continuous measurement of production...

Kind of creepy, isn't it? It's true we are no longer training people for factory work. It's the twenty-first century and most of the factories have disappeared from the US, along with the salaries that enabled large numbers of Americans to join the middle class. But we still have a *factory model* of schooling.

We tend to take for granted that schools are the way they are for good reasons. Many of the "givens" of schooling—the sorting of children by age into grades and by ability level into "tracks," the awarding of units of credit, letter grades, the division of the day into periods—are so familiar that it is hard to imagine things differently. But such reforms were specific responses to perceived problems, instituted by people with power and authority and sustained by custom and the inertia of large institutions. All of these innovations were influenced by the social efficiency movement, which was guided by elites who attempted to model social functions such as education after the model of factory production. The guru of scientific management was Frederick Taylor, who developed such ideas as the standardization of production, the speed of labor inputs, quality control on the production line, and small incentives designed to overcome the natural slothfulness of agrarian peasants and turn them into industrial workers. School administrators took to Taylor's ideas with gusto, for the factory model solved many key organizational and administrative problems.

Factory production, whether of cornflakes or jet planes, generally involves the shaping of raw materials into products on a conveyor belt. Schools, as Cubberly suggested, take the raw materials—children—and move them along the conveyor belt of classrooms and curriculum with the end goal being an educated person, which today means someone who can memorize large amounts of information and successfully pass tests.

Factories require the standardization of tools and machinery. In education, standardization is a no-brainer from the standpoint of conventional wisdom. The current standards movement went into overdrive in the early 1980's with the publication of *A Nation at Risk*, a national commission report that frightened the American public with dire threats to "our once unchallenged preeminence in commerce, industry, science, and technological innovation" from other industrialized countries. Governors and states got involved, and for the past few decades, policy makers have been obsessed with standards, measurement, and accountability, with little evidence that schools have actually improved, or that there is any demonstrated causal relationship between national learning standards and economic competitiveness.

A standards-based educational system means that some body of individuals (usually politicians, bureaucrats, and business leaders) sets learning goals and objectives for students, grade by grade, and specifies the skills and information to be acquired at each level. Common standards are a form of quality control—we want all mass-produced products to look, feel, and taste the same as the last item we bought. We don't want our ketchup to be sweeter than usual, or our cornflakes to be less crunchy. Teachers, students, and schools are held accountable for making progress according to these externally imposed standards. Failure to do so results in severe penalties: grade retention for students, failing marks for schools, and the ever-present possibility that the staff will be fired and the school eliminated or reorganized. The demand to build students to these specifications—Cubberly again—has resulted in rampant teaching to the test, a form of instruction that focuses on the acquisition of discrete skills and bits of information, largely divorced from meaning or relevance. It has also sparked a number of cheating scandals implicating entire large school districts. Currently, the standards movement finds its apotheosis in the adoption of Common Core Learning Standards in English and math, kindergarten through twelfth grade, in all but a shrinking handful of states. These resisters will probably soon follow suit, if they wish to acquire the highly competitive grant money that the feds are offering as an incentive. Given the frantic pace of education policy change, even the Common Core may soon be replaced by other standards; what is not likely to change is the effort by elites to standardize and control what all children must learn.

In a factory, the emphasis is on productivity. Though productivity technically means turning out the same product with less labor, for schools it usually translates to more seat time and more stringent attendance policies—the longer a student is sitting in school, it is assumed, the greater the learning that takes place. Bruising teacher-union contract negotiations sometimes result in an extra four minutes a day spent on instruction, as if such seat time could ever result in a measurable difference in the quality of learning!

In a factory, there is a clear hierarchy, an organizational model of centralized decision-making and top-down control, despite occasional efforts to institute models of self-managed production teams and other job-enrichment techniques. And despite twentieth-century experiments in site-based management and other organizational reforms, the education business is now more hierarchical than ever. Standards are imposed from the political level, policies come top down through the educational bureaucracy, and power is wielded over teachers by cadres of administrators, coaches, and supervisors who are assessing compliance in everything from making sure the teacher is reading from the right page of the curriculum script to how far off the floor the word wall is taped. I am not exaggerating, and things are getting worse in this respect, not better. Schools, after all, must enforce rules to maintain smooth assembly-line procedures. Teachers subjected to such close monitoring find it necessary to monitor their students ever more carefully for *their* compliance, leaving little room for imagination, creativity, pleasure, social interaction, or the personalization of learning. Their jobs depend upon it!

Historically speaking, the shift from an artisan society in which workers generally saw their products through from conception to completion (think about potters, weavers, chefs, or furniture builders) to a factory-based system in which workers were only responsible for turning a screw or sewing in a zipper was not met with universal enthusiasm. Strikes and riots over wages and working conditions were common. While artisans had a fair amount of control over their time and could engage in a satisfying variety of tasks, the regimented work of the factory ate away at the soul. Only the external incentive of a wage sustained workers through boredom, repetitive stress injuries, and constant injunctions to speed up. Factory schools, as well, get results (short-term ones at least) through incentives—everything from gold stars, grades, pizza parties, and promotions to merit pay and tenure for teachers whose students score well on tests.

Of course the standardization of school practices, the grouping of children by age, or ability, or IQ scores, and the division of knowledge into prescribed bits, easily digested and tested, brought a measure of efficiency to schools, and over time these innovations became widely accepted. The problem with the factory model, however, is that students are not products and they generally don't respond positively to a culture that treats them as if they were cars on an assembly line. The mandate to teach all students in a cohort the same material at the same pace does not account for human differences, and a vast new array of problems emerged with factory schooling: students whose profile did not match the norm were labeled as slow, retarded, mentally deficient, and deviant. They often became dropouts (as high as 97% at the beginning of the twentieth century and between 16% and 24% now, depending on which figures you cite—and that rate goes up to 50% in some of our largest cities). Today we have fancy labels for students who don't conform to school practices: emotionally disturbed, behaviorally challenged, oppositional defiant, etc. Indeed, there are children with challenging emotional issues related to abuse and neglect, as well as children with serious neurological disorders, and these can play out in troubling ways in schools. But this book starts from the premise that the way schools are structured is a significant contributing factor in many behaviors that get labeled as deviant, and further, that the factory model of schooling, no matter how much we tinker with it, will never result in the kind of learning that is required for the complex society of today.

I am not alone in these conclusions. Between 1.5 and 2.5 million families in the United States have taken the dramatic step of opting out of public *and* private schools and assuming the enormous challenges of homeschooling or *unschooling* their children. These terms are not quite interchangeable. Homeschooling merely suggests that kids are being educated outside a formal school setting, usually under the guidance of their parents. The curriculum of the homeschool may be every bit as formal and structured as that of the public school. Unschoolers tend to reject the entire apparatus of school, and the paradigm on which it is based, which claims to anticipate the skills and knowledge children will need to know in the future, and attempts to impart these whether or not the children are interested. Unschooling implies an embrace of the idea that children are naturally curious, meaning-seeking creatures with interests and concerns that should be allowed to guide their learning. There are probably as many reasons for homeschooling and unschooling as there are families who choose to do it. People seek educational alternatives for a variety of reasons: the desire to instill a particular religious perspective; worries about sex, drugs, and violence in schools; concerns that schools are overly focused on teaching to the test. Scratch below the surface of these differences and you discover that most families who exercise these choices want their children to enjoy learning and become independent thinkers, self-reliant workers, and creative problem-solvers. Sure there are well-publicized exceptions—parents who institute more rigid and regimented schooling practices than the factory schools. But my guess is that most of the parents who opt out of school care deeply about the development of their children, and have nagging doubts that institutionalized education can ever meet their child's distinctive needs, unleash their full potential, or nurture their spirituality.

Homeschooling may seem like a retro idea, and indeed, much of the publicity surrounding it evokes images of the frontier family—children sitting at Mom's feet reading Bible verses. But increasingly, some version of unschooling has become a compelling option for contemporary parents—rural, urban, suburban, black, white, middle class, working class parents—who sense that the current fixation on common standards, rote learning, and over testing threatens to dull the minds and passions of an entire generation of young people. And perhaps they have a sneaking suspicion that the brick and mortar concept of school, with its restricted ways of organizing space, time, relationships, work, and the flow of information, is an outdated and inadequate template for learning in the twenty-first century.

I was once one of these parents. And although my journey into and through unschooling was as quirky as the next person's, I think I shared with most parents a set of passionately held beliefs about what my children might hope for from their educations:

~ My child is an absolutely unique expression of human *being*. He is not an interchangeable part on an assembly line.

~ My child has unlimited potential; education should foster his dreams and talents.

~ There is a deep well of creativity lurking in my child. Educational experiences should call this forth.

~ My child has a timetable that is his or her own. I believe that his learning should be paced to match that, not the other way around.

~ My child has ideas that are important; I want him to feel free to express them, and to expect that he will be listened to respectfully.

~ My child's social, emotional, and spiritual development is as essential as his academic learning.

~ I want my child to experience the deep pleasure that is inherent in learning about the world; learning should not be seen as drudgery or punishment.

~ I want my child to master skills that are important to him, and which enable him to succeed in life.

~ There are a zillion interesting things to learn about; I want my child to exercise choice over what he will study.

~ It is important to me that my child becomes a responsible member of the community; I want him to care about other people, plants, animals, the well-being of the earth, and the state of the world. I want his learning to foster this care, as well as awe, wonder, curiosity, appreciation, sensitivity, and a dedication to life-long learning.

These were my fundamentals. My four boys are all grown now, all of them middle-aged, with families of their own. Enough time has elapsed that I can lay claim to that most valuable form of knowledge—the wisdom of hindsight. These essays were authored by numerous authors, all inhabiting my own body. There is Young Me, a free spirit who abandoned a career in show business to plunge headfirst into the counterculture of the 1960's, riding a motorcycle across America seeking whatever it was people were seeking back then. There is Alternative Education Me, finding meaning and purpose in the heady world of educational experimentation embodied by the free school movement. There is Earth Mother Me, married and struggling to raise four boys against the grain of the consumer culture and keep the idealism of the counterculture alive. And last, there is Scholar Me, the product of a couple of graduate degrees in education and thirty years as a university educator who has conducted research, sat on numerous policy commissions, and worked with thousands of teachers, student teachers, and school leaders to help them become thoughtful about the enormously important task they have in guiding and shaping the lives of young people.

These voices are sometimes at odds with each other. Scholar Me is sometimes embarrassed by the other Me's, with their naïve idealism, or unreflective individualism, or their untempered belief in freedom. But I have tried to let them all live here, and the reader can sort out for themselves which Me thought what and when. Memory is an elusive thing, shaped and reshaped by experience. But just as the past is inextricably interwoven with the present, the threads of my early convictions are part of the warp and weave of my more developed thinking. The stories are all true, recorded in the journals I kept for the five years that we unschooled. They are as real as I can make them, my "boys" having kept me firmly attached to reality as they read through portions of the book and told me in no uncertain terms when my recall or my interpretation was flawed.

This book is dedicated to them, but also to the multitude of parents out there who want the best for their kids and have a nagging sense that one-size-fits-all education does not fit anybody. And it is dedicated to the large number of teachers who turn screws and press levers in the education factory and know in their hearts that there is a better way. Most of all, it is dedicated to the idea that all kids should be nourished and supported by adults who believe in their unlimited potential to become purposeful, responsible, creative, compassionate, and contented human beings who never want to stop learning about the world they live in.

Prologue

IN MY DREAM, I rake rocks back and forth across the dirt road that leads to the old stone shack on Stick Ross Mountain. I pick them up, one at a time, and examine their striation. Each holds its own glacial story. I unearth long buried scraps of fabric, and in their disintegrating threads, I see the remnants of faded plaids and paisleys. I reconstruct objects from scattered bits and pieces of metal and plastic and wood that only gradually reveal their partial forms. This work of remembering is a painstaking excavation, an archaeology of the soul.

Stick Ross Mountain
1971

MY CROTCH BONES ARE killing me and it feels like both kidneys have been permanently relocated. I am traveling on the back of a BMW motorcycle, my arms locked around Stretch's skinny waist, my face burrowed into his long black hair. My boyfriend is six foot four inches of California-tanned gorgeousness, and he has just been dishonorably discharged from the army for something having to do with a plan to smuggle medical supplies to North Vietnam from the base at San Luis Obispo. I am wildly in love, sufficiently smitten to ride atop seven hundred pounds of organ-damaging, ear-numbing metal through blistering southwestern desert sun, sweating Mississippi Delta sharecropper country, and monsoon-style Florida rains for weeks. We are Easy Riding refugees from the disintegration of the West Coast love and drug fest of the late 1960's. I'm what's known as a Hollywood gypsy. I make my living dancing on television, and in movies, operas, musical comedies, and grand Nevada casino showrooms. He's a bass-playing rocker, yearning to work the big time arenas, but mostly stuck in Las Vegas and Long Beach lounges; at least he was until his number came up in the draft lottery. Then he got stuck in the army.

I am hungry much of the time on the road because Stretch, under the influence of a nineteenth-century naturopath named Arnold Ehret who believed that humans should only consume foods that fall from trees, has decided that we will be fruitarians. I am hungry even when we sleep in avocado orchards and eat our fill of the fatty fruit. I am hungry even after he decides it is okay for us to have trail mix. But I don't mind being hungry because

I am so wildly in love. And I am wonderfully thin and I like the feeling of the wind blowing my long dark hair out in back of me as we ride and it feels good to be young and handsome and sexy and in love and part of the huge nomadic swath of Baby Boomers crisscrossing the country, discovering America Kerouac-style.

We leave Fort Lauderdale hastily one dawn with the police pounding on the front door of the communal rock and roll house where we are staying. It occurs to me that perhaps the band has been selling the grass that was so abundant in this house. On the other hand, it is not unusual for police to just bust into houses that have long-haired hippies living in them. We don't stick around to learn the details. Jamming our one change of clothes, the trail mix, and the Arnold Ehret books into our backpacks, we climb out a first-story back window, strap everything onto the BMW, and hightail it out of the tropics as they bust the door down. We decide to head straight for Oklahoma, so Stretch can return to his roots in Indian country. *Goin' to get back to the land, goin' to set our souls free.*

Tahlequah, Oklahoma, the capital of the Cherokee Nation, is a foreign land to me, with its dirt roads, Depression-era sandstone buildings, and old-time general store that sells tin buckets and hand plows and canning jars. Stretch's mom and dad and Leslie, his developmentally delayed grown brother, live outside of town at the base of Stick Ross Mountain in a weathered white clapboard house, and nine or ten other siblings are scattered between here and west Texas. Stretch's dad was a teacher at the local Indian high school until he retired some twenty years ago. His mom gave birth to Leslie in her sixties and she is no spring chicken. They are all very overweight, and she wears button-down-the-front housedresses and lace up black shoes with thick heels like my great grandmother wore in the 1930's. She tries to feed us things like grits and biscuits, which sure smell good to me, but we are fruitarians and so of course averse to mucus-forming foods. I can't wrap my head around the idea that this family and this place is where my handsome, hip California rocker boyfriend comes from.

We probably look as foreign to the townsfolk as this whole scene looks to me, with our flowing hair, animal-skin vests, moccasins, and beaded feather and bone jewelry. Never mind that our attire is vaguely Indian and just about everyone here is some portion Indian; actual Indians haven't dressed like this for at least a century. The Manson murders are fresh in everybody's mind, even out here in the hinterlands, and folks get the jitters now when they see hippies. Stretch's older brother Joe gets the jitters so bad, he fires a shotgun at Stretch one day when he rides the BMW into town. Not exactly a roaring welcome home.

I am so wildly in love I don't mind that the old stone shack on Stick Ross Mountain that one of Stretch's clan lets us stay in only has glass in a couple of its windows or that it is breathtakingly filthy thanks to the two traveling peddlers who have been squatting in it. I am surprised to learn that peddlers exist outside of nineteenth-century English novels. From the look and smell of things, these two entertained themselves by smashing small whiskey bottles and tossing raw eggs at each other. We take scrub brushes and Dr. Bronner's soap to every surface and soon the place smells sweetly of peppermint and pot (just a wee bit of the latter, because we are busy detoxifying, à la Arnold Ehret, who surely would have disapproved). Crosby, Stills, Nash and Young play the soundtrack in my mind...

Our House....is a very very very fine house.
With two cats in the yard. Life used to be so hard.
Now everything is easy 'cause of you...

...and in the movie trailer that runs in my head we will plant a garden and fix up this house real nice, with homemade curtains and a wood-burning stove. We will weave and stitch and decorate our own clothes and read books and write poetry and songs for the acoustic guitar, meditate, and live a life of Oneness with Nature.

Until now, my working model of Nature has consisted of the ornamental tree-shrubs and velvety-green grass of Golden Gate

Park, or perhaps the pristine Northern California Redwood forest where my mom and dad and I used to summer. But Nature here is tangled and scrubby and dense and chaotic. Oklahoma awakens something wild in me, its syrupy spring nights bursting with a cacophony of unfamiliar sounds. Screeching, chirping, scurrying, howling, hooting—through those gaping window holes an endless variety of nonhuman voices echo in my civilized ears.

In the long, hot, dry summer, I sometimes imagine that I am made of red Oklahoma clay, a twentieth-century female golem. As I strive to become One With Nature, I visualize my body loosening its boundaries, so that where I end and the earth begins is not clear. These might be protein-starved hallucinations. I am, after all, still hungry, even though we consume entire Oklahoma watermelons at a sitting, and they are the sweetest and juiciest I have ever eaten. We have little energy for much besides doing yoga and swimming in the murky pond reached by a trail that we scythe through the woods. I throw stones in the water and contemplate the ripples that spread out in magically concentric circles. This seems profound.

Like squirrels, we spend the autumn gathering black walnuts that stain our hands, and tiny wild pecans that are impossible to dig out of their shells. We are so poor that we qualify for government commodities, but when we go through the box in the white clapboard house at the base of Stick Ross Mountain, we discover that the only things we can eat are the peanut butter and the raisins. And even the peanuts are cheating, according to the good Professor Ehret, for they do not fall from trees. We hand over the big block of American cheese food and the farina and the canned meat to Stretch's family. Stretch tells me that many of the Cherokee and other tribal people around here believe that the government puts saltpeter in the commodities as part of a program to sterilize the Indians. Perhaps it's true. We've been fasting a lot, and to our sharpened senses, the canned and processed food has a nasty vibe. But I dream about cheese sandwiches for weeks afterward.

We buy a bushel of freshly harvested apples with our meager cash reserves so that we can eat seasonally in the coming cold months. Being a seasonal fruitarian in a Florida or Oklahoma summer has been a lush lark, but I anticipate that being one in a Midwestern winter will not be for the faint of heart. We pick persimmons after the first frost, which really taste like crap. Stretch ferments them in stone crocks, convinced that Arnold Ehret would approve of wild, organic wine. He tapes clear plastic over the window holes and covers the stone floor with straw, both of us blissfully unaware that spiders and snakes will find this a delightful winter haven. We buy a tin wood stove at the general store for about twenty bucks, and a cord of wood from a local preacher for fifteen, which we stack neatly against the front of the house. *Our house. A very very very fine house.*

We really do have two cats in the yard, black ones, strays that found their way to us in the spring. They've found their way to each other as well, and by winter there have been two litters. We now have thirteen black cats in the yard. Stretch's mom tells us that the folks in the backwoods, none of whom we have laid eyes on, think we are witches. Maybe we are. We light candles and perform our mail-order Rosicrucian lessons that promise to teach us to "access your own source of inner wisdom and guidance" in the ways of the Mystery Schools of ancient Egypt. We dance naked in the moonlight and in the rain. But it soon gets too cold for such cavorting. So we stare at the fire...*for hours and hours...While I listen to you play your love songs all night long for me...ee...ee..ee... Only for me.* The tin stove glows a devilish orange when it gets to cooking and I am terrified that the whole thing is going to explode while we are sleeping and catch the straw on fire.

When it gets very, very cold in our very fine house, Stretch decides that what he really wants is not to be One With Nature, but to be a Rock Star. I could come along, of course, but I remind him that I didn't sign on for the life of a groupie. I signed on to get back to the land and to set my soul free. He leaves me with the bushel baskets of apples and pecans and black walnuts, and heads off on the BMW to Tulsa and on to Los Angeles and back to sunny Florida to the communal rock and roll house and God knows where else. We don't have a telephone so I rarely hear from him. Occasionally he calls the family home, and Leslie drives up the road to fetch me. It's the seventies, and we are supposed to be practicing free love and nonattachment, but I am truly heartbroken.

I am also six miles from the nearest town, on rough dirt roads. There are no other dwellings within shouting distance. I have no transportation. I have no money save for a forty-seven-dollar unemployment check that gets delivered by the US Post Office once a month to Stretch's family's house. The postman doesn't come up this far. Stretch drops in unexpectedly a couple of times this winter with an entourage that includes starry-eyed females. He wows them with bottles of his home-brewed persimmon wine. It tastes like vinegar and piss to me. He expects I've kept the home fires burning. The tin stove still glows but my fire is out and there is a stone in my chest. We both move on. I'm just not sure where I'm moving on to yet.

~

By dumb luck or sheer survival instinct, I make it through the lonely winter. I buy myself some lumberjack boots with a good fraction of one of my unemployment checks, and spend every morning splitting oak and cedar logs. Afterwards, I drink herb tea at the rickety wooden table by the window where the weak morning sun shines in. A large brown spider with a belly full of eggs weaves and reweaves her silvery web there each day. I marvel at her persistence. Afternoons, I sit shivering by a frugal fire that smolders in the tin stove, painstakingly picking nutmeats out of their shells with numb fingers. Stretch's mom and Leslie occasionally drive up the mountain and bring me bananas. I spread them with commodity peanut butter and raisins, and am grateful. Nights, I build up the fire, read by the light of our one kerosene lamp, and make mystical mandalas by sewing teeny Victorian glass beads onto the twenty-five-cents-a-yard unbleached muslin that I buy at the general store when I get my boots.

A solitary witch turns out to be less terrifying to the superstitious locals than a pair of witches. One night I am meditating by candlelight, practicing my Rosicrucian lessons. I am still a Neophyte but I have graduated from Mystical Sounds and Cosmic Consciousness and moved on to Visualization and Telepathy. I hear the sound of hooves galloping in the yard. Through the plastic film on the windows, I see men on horses, about six or eight of them. It's hard to tell how many because they are riding around and around the house. They are shouting and I can't understand their words, but I know it does not bode well. Gunshots puncture the cold night air. One part of me is thinking this is too surreal, like something out of the primal past. Can't possibly be happening. Another part of me knows the men are genuine flesh and blood and I experience a bone-freezing fear like I have seldom known before. I am sure they have come to kill or at least rape and mutilate me. On some level I know that they are frightened of me and that is why they are behaving like outlaws at the O.K. Corral. I also sense that if I let them know I am afraid they will lose their fear and truly hurt me. So I raise my arms and my eyes to the ceiling, summon my budding Rosicrucian Powers of Thought and Concentration, not to mention my theatrical training, and simply sit there, immobile. The lone candle flickers. Let them think I am casting the darkest of spells. They circle the house a few more times, hooting and hollering, and then ride away.

The next day I awaken from a troubled sleep with the deep and sure knowledge that I am way too isolated. I resolve to remedy this and begin to make tentative excursions into town. When I hitch rides into Tahlequah I wear a pearl-handled dagger in a leather sheath that Stretch made for me. I don't know what I will do if someone actually attacks me, as I have no clue how to defend myself with a knife, but I take comfort in the strong message it sends. I have learned an important lesson about fear. The chirpy tune from *Anna and the King of Siam* plays in my head.

Whenever I feel afraid,
I hold my head erect
and whistle a happy tune
and no one will suspect I'm afraid.

As it turns out there are some like-minded souls in this god-forsaken place. I meet an extended family of Wenatchee/Flathead Indians who take me under their collective wing. I become good friends with the four daughters and develop a mild crush on the son, who happens to be my age and is just back from Vietnam. It is clear that I have a genetic predisposition to very tall, handsome men with black hair streaming down their backs. At least he is not a musician. But it is their mother who really interests me. Mrs. George, the matriarch of the family, is well acquainted with Rosicrucian lore and the teachings of theosophy as well. I eagerly enlist her as my spiritual teacher. Enough of mail-order lessons. I don't really care about ancient Egyptians anyway. This is the real thing. The family is an autonomous group of the Native American Church, and they welcome me into the experience of peyote tea and the ritual of the sweat lodge. I have, but for minor lapses, forsworn psychedelics. But there is something here to learn, and I drink deeply.

The lodge is a small, round, dome-shaped structure in the woods out back of the home of a clan member. It is made of supple willow branches and covered over with tarps and blankets. On the night of my first sweat, I walk down the trail with the four daughters, Mrs. George, and another woman I have just met. Two young children of the oldest daughter are with us. Sonny, the object of my crush, is heating rocks in a fire pit outside the lodge. He's been at it all afternoon. It's an honorable role, to be the fire keeper, and fraught with some sort of spiritual significance that I have yet to fully understand. I move with the women into the lodge, as I have been taught, holy naked. It feels like I am crawling deep into the earth. I can only see vague outlines but I hear the breathing of the others. We sit on straw. Mrs. George sprinkles water from a ladle onto the glowing rocks that have been placed in a pit in the center and I experience a gradual skin-sizzling, lung-bursting heat. Sonny occasionally passes in a fresh rock with a pitchfork through the ground level opening, which raises the heat index considerably. We flog ourselves with cedar branches to drive the impurities away. We pray, we sing, and there is some joke telling too. The water pours off me, shedding my youthful sins and cleansing my soul. It is like nothing I have ever experienced and I feel like I have truly *gotten back to the land and set my soul free.*

I spend many days in Mrs. George's sunny living room, and she patiently teaches me what she knows about the mysteries of reincarnation and mental projection. But what I really learn from her is far more important. In my white, western, middle-class, urban/suburban, never-trust-anyone-over-thirty life experience, I have never met a family who all appear to be on the same wavelength, with no indication of a generation gap. In my heart, I know this will shape my future. For the first time ever, I begin to develop the stirrings of maternal instinct. I want a family with this level of intimacy and connection. But my boyfriend has run off to be a Rock Star and my crush on Sonny, which really is more of an attraction to the entire extended family than to him, is for the most part, unrequited.

My unemployment checks run out. Paltry as they are, they have kept me in candles and kerosene and trail mix. Though the logical next step for a fruitarian is to become a *breatharian*, and live on light and air alone, I admit to myself that I am hopelessly earthbound. If I am to survive, I need to find an entry to the local cash economy.

The *Help Wanted* section of the newspaper makes me weep. While I am skilled at navigating Hollywood auditions and Central Casting, and have managed to stay steadily employed in the dance world, I have no marketable skills for the mainstream economy. Especially the rural mainstream economy. Besides, the jobs available are so depressing to my artistic soul that I consider getting a bus ticket back to the West Coast. But I don't *want* to go back to that scene; there are deep and complicated reasons why I fled. I am intrigued with this new life and enjoy exploring a world that was completely off my mental map. Besides, I don't have the price of a bus ticket.

I land a job as a waitress at a local steak and hamburger joint on Muskogee Ave., the main street in Tahlequah. I walk down the mountain and hitch a ride into town each day. I am reasonably competent at getting the orders right and not spilling any trays of food. But a year of fruit eating and water fasting has made it impossible to bear the relentless smell of burning flesh. I quit a couple of weeks in.

There is a bar across the street from the hamburger joint. I can do this, fill beer glasses, pour shots, collect tips. I get the job. I don't know which is worse, the stench of burning flesh or the reek of stale beer and cigarettes, but I am determined to give this my best shot. It is slow in the bar the first couple of days, the occasional farmer stopping in for a cold beer, or the town boozer keeping the stool at the end of the bar warm. I have plenty of time to learn the ropes, which are relatively simple. Open the draft faucet, hold the glass at a forty-five-degree angle, bring it slowly to a vertical position, lower it a bit to create a head. Set it down in front of the customer, take the money (no tabs), give change. Find the owner if someone gets belligerent or throws up or falls. No brains required.

Friday comes. It is the day of the month when the welfare checks arrive in mailboxes. Men stream in wearing mud-caked boots and cowboy hats. The place fills up before noon. Not a woman in sight. I am racing from one end of the bar to the other, pouring shots, filling beer glasses like a pro. A man pulls out a handgun and slides it down the bar to me. Then another man slams a gun down, and another. Aghast, I look around for the owner, who has stepped out. The men are pointing at some place behind the bar and laughing. I am freaking out. All I can think of are the horseback riders circling my shack, firing their guns. The owner comes in the front door, lifts up the counter hinge and comes behind the bar, takes a key from his ring and opens the drawer that the men are pointing at. This is the gun drawer and it's a firm rule in this joint. All guns go in the drawer.

The closest I have ever come to the wild west was in a few episodes of a television show by that name, *The Wild Wild West*, and *Gunsmoke*, where I always played a saloon girl. And my desk mate at Hollywood High School in geography was Johnny Crawford, of *Rifleman* fame. Other than that, my world has not included real men with guns. I make it through Saturday night and give my notice.

By now, I have made friends in town. The George clan is well extended into the community, and I hang out with people around my age who are raising families and working or who attend the nearby college. The sixties have come late to this part of the country, but these folks have long hair and like to sit around and play acoustic music together, smoke a bit of pot, and live a generally laid-back lifestyle, which is easy to do in this sleepy place. It's an innocent version of the cultural revolution; a bit of the spirit without the chaos and craziness. I am somewhat alien to the local hippies, with my weird diet and my pearl-handled dagger, my long skirts and my mysterious Haight Ashbury/Hollywood past, but I am warmly accepted. One night we are gathered at Bill and Linda's house and someone brings out the local newspaper.

"Check this out! They're having auditions for summer theater jobs up at the college on Saturday."

My ears perk up. Theater jobs? Turns out there is a Cherokee Cultural Center less than three miles from Stick Ross Mountain with a living museum and a big amphitheater where they put on a lavish summer re-enactment of the Trail of Tears, the genocidal march that relocated thousands of Cherokee from their homeland in Georgia out to the desolate Indian Territory. Northeast Oklahoma was the end of the line for those who survived. They are looking for singers and dancers and actors.

I attend the audition in the gym, which is overrun with college coeds, and go through the paces with Marvin, the choreographer. Marvin is the first truly familiar soul I have run into in a long time, a dancing gay Jew from New York. I haven't been out of commission long enough to completely lose my chops, as they say in the business, and this is far and away the least demanding audition I have ever been to, a few simple ballet combinations. It is not a major challenge to stand out from the crowd. Auditioning and performing, after all, is what I do. Just about all I have ever done, besides teaching dance. Marvin chooses a pack of us to stay, sends the rest home, and then asks each of us in turn if we have ever been in a show before. When he calls my name, I give him the short list. People stare at me. He calls me up to his table.

"What the hell are you doing in Tahlequah?" he asks, with a truly puzzled look on his face.

"I could ask you the same thing," I respond.

We become instant friends, and I am hired on the spot. It is a fraction of what I have earned in the past — only $75 a week. But it is cash money and it is for dancing and I will no longer have to bear the smells of burning flesh or stale beer.

~

The summer that I playact the part of a Cherokee maiden who survived the Trail of Tears is the summer I get a crash course in the plight of real native people in the US. It's not that I haven't been exposed to politics. One could hardly avoid them in California in the late sixties. But my participation has been peripheral. Once, right after the Watts riots in 1965, I was working for free in an independent film about teenagers run amok in a post-apocalyptic world. This was a truly low-budget affair, and a day or so after the fiery mêlée, the filmmaker gleefully piled us indie actors, in our mini-skirts and knee-high boots, blue jeans and T-shirts, into a big rented van along with the equipment and crew of two. Driving south from Hollywood, we careened through police blockades and milling throngs into the war zone that was Watts and then spent an hour or so scampering through smoldering ruins for the handheld cameras. I had another close encounter with urban battle and flames in 1968, when I was performing in Chicago. I was at an after-show party with jazz musicians on the old north side when the news came of riots in the city following the assassination of MLK. We looked out the apartment window to a city ringed with fire. Trying to make my way home, I was nearly run over by the National Guard in an armored vehicle while sniper fire rang overhead. Wild times, but I was more of an onlooker than a participant.

When I lived in California, I preferred reading *The San Francisco Oracle* over the *Berkeley Barb*, a fact that means something only if you were there during the heyday of the cultural revolution. *The Oracle*, with its fabulous psychedelic graphics and esoteric poetry, fed my aesthetic and spiritual self. The *Barb*, with its political diatribes, raised my consciousness but didn't inspire me to action. This summer, however, I learn from the actors who are more politically conscious than me that the white people in the drama earn significantly more than the brown people. And I learn that the actual historical events have been "whitewashed" in this made-for-tourists production. On the closing night of the show, tribal and government dignitaries join a large crowd to celebrate a successful theater season. Television crews are on hand for this major public event. And here we performers are, in front of the entrance, carrying signs and placards protesting wage injustice. The producer seethes. There is a rumor that something pretty exciting is going to happen in the drama tonight. And indeed, something exciting does happen. A couple of the actors have rewritten major parts of the play in a way that highlights the genocide and oppression of the Cherokee, rather than the happy assimilation and jubilant statehood celebration featured in the summer production. There are cars waiting out back to spirit away the ringleaders after the final curtain. They disappear and the producer comes backstage and rants at the rest of us, hollering that none of us can hope to ever, EVER be hired again for this show. But that's okay, because I have found a new passion, in the intersecting worlds of art and education and politics.

~

Through the George family, I have met Dave, a smallish man with rimless glasses who wears Levis and tweed jackets with elbow patches and smokes a tobacco pipe, and his wife Maggie, an appealingly wacky art teacher at the local college. Dave has gotten himself fired for trying to organize a chapter of the Black Panthers on the local Tahlequah college campus, where he was a social science professor with tenure. A former minister and a Ph.D. candidate at the Union Graduate School, he is now designing and directing an alternative undergraduate degree granting institution for his doctoral project and he is doing this right on the doorstep of the institution that terminated his contract. Dave is a man with a vision, and he effortlessly recruits some of us untethered creative types into his project. A few more radical souls are imported from Goddard College in Vermont, an academic bastion of progressive politics. Uncle River is a graduate of Goddard who has recently finished his Ph.D. coursework at the Jung Institute in Switzerland and he is keen to analyze our dreams. Kent is a Goddard graduate who builds boats; he and I enjoy a brief flirtation until I discover he has a very un-hippie-like temper. Marianne is a hefty, self-proclaimed witch of the north with long flowing red hair and a black cape who has a great deal of administrative experience working as a registrar or some such thing at Goddard. She does not like me very much, I can tell. Once she visits the house on Stick Ross Mountain with Uncle River, who she used to be in a relationship with, and Kent, who she would like to be in a relationship with, and at the sight of a daddy longlegs gracefully stepping across the floor, leaps up on a chair and will not come down. She doesn't last long in Oklahoma. We affiliate with the University Without Walls network, part of a consortium of experimenting colleges and universities. Change is in the air and we are energetically committed to bringing it about.

We spend intense days and nights debating educational philosophy and social theory, studying the *Foxfire* books, and reading *Pedagogy of the Oppressed*, which has just been published in English. I fit right into this interesting and slightly disaffected crowd. Many in our group are Native American, and we study indigenous history, folklore, and arts and crafts from local elders, just like in the *Foxfire* experiment. We get to know AIM activists from the Pine Ridge reservation and we support the revolutionary revival of Native American cultures. Inspired by a vision of Black Elk, an Oglala Sioux survivor of the Battle of Wounded Knee, we name our UWW center Flaming Rainbow University. Magically, Dave obtains BIA and veteran's funding for students. I am neither an Indian nor a veteran, and have no money to speak of, but I get hired as a staff advisor with tuition remission. The pay is nonexistent but the satisfactions are enormous. To be changing the world is no small thing. And, to top it off, we gain regional accreditation, which makes us legit.

In return for the various kinds of work I do, everything from cooking vegetarian food for hundreds of people at alternative education conferences to typing reports to staging an antiwar rock musical in the local college theater (which was raided by the local police), I have the opportunity to finish my BA degree through this alternative institution. I am awarded numerous credits for "prior life experience": in my case, the years I spent at a prestigious professional school in Hollywood studying every conceivable style of dance, in addition to more academic subjects such as kinesiography (dance notation), choreography, dramatic movement, music theory, and dance history.

I am a book junkie. Always have been. When I was a dancer, I spent every spare dime at the Pickwick Bookshop on the corner of Hollywood and Vine on my weekly fix of reading material. I read promiscuously, developing crushes on authors—Doris Lessing, Kurt Vonnegut, J.D. Salinger, Upton Sinclair, John Updike—that lasted until I had exhausted their work. There was no rhyme or reason to my choices. I had fervent affairs with Richard Wright and Bertrand Russell and Isaac Asimov and Jane Austen and Krishnamurti and James Baldwin and Karl Marx and Simone de Beauvoir and St. Thomas Aquinas. I read during rehearsals when I was not needed on stage. I read in musty dressing rooms between shows. No one ever suggested that all this reading might be channeled into a college education. The adults in my life always figured I would be a famous dancer and most likely marry a rich man. No one questioned my destiny, except for the wardrobe lady in the Golden Hotel Casino, who once, as she zipped me into my costume, read my palm, and said, "Whoa –your palm says very clearly that you are not a dancer, you are a writer." But now I not only have free rein to read what I wish, I am even getting college credit for it. I cast my net wide: religion, philosophy, anthropology, folklore, myth, literature, ecology, feminism, nutrition, organic farming, and education theory. I discover and document the knowledge embedded in everyday events, whether it is building a new sweat lodge, attending a powwow, constructing a geodesic dome, organizing a conference, or exploring the socio-spiritual-historical implications of mescaline. This is everything school should be but isn't: absolutely relevant to my current interests, designed by me, rooted in place and community, and oriented towards the creation of a better world. Besides that, it is FUN! We are having a great time discovering that learning can actually be pleasurable, not the dreary and punishing experience we had been led to believe it was doomed to be.

One day, I am walking down the block in front of the storefront we have rented for Flaming Rainbow's offices and "classrooms" (most of our learning takes place in the real world, not in stuffy rooms), on my way to teach the free ballet class I offer to low-income children in the community. Standing at the door is—uh-oh—a tall, good-looking guy with black hair streaming down his back. It is late summer, approaching the start of a new fall semester at the local college and Earl has returned home from a life of political activism in Berkeley to enroll in a teacher education program so that he can teach history. But he has gotten sidetracked here at the door of Flaming Rainbow, a group of radical hippies and an alternative university the last things he expected to find in Tahlequah. He joins us at Bill and Linda's house that evening, where we all sit around the small living room and play bongos and guitars and tambourines. He sits behind me and caresses my hair. He is quiet and tender and gentle with smoldering eyes that hint of a great spiritual fire within.

Earl was born in San Bernadino, California, descended from Okies, many of them Cherokee, who joined the exodus to California when their land dried up and blew away back in the 1930s. But he grew up in Oklahoma, and he might have stayed here had he not had some bruising encounters with the Oklahoma City police when he tried to organize an OKC chapter of Vietnam Veterans Against the War. He tells me the story of how he left Oklahoma late one night after one friend of his was shot by the authorities and another beat up by them in an elevator, and how, upon being told in no uncertain terms to leave the state, he was followed by the cops all the way to the New Mexico border. In California, he hangs out at People's Park, takes part in protests and meets Eldridge Cleaver by accident when he runs into an open door in a back alley during a protest-turned-riot in Oakland—and finds himself in the middle of a Black Panthers meeting. It is inevitable that we begin to spend time together. It is also inevitable that Earl will use his hard won GI benefits to attend Flaming Rainbow University rather than the local campus. And it is probably inevitable that I eventually offer him, rent-free, the one-room unfinished-wood cabin that sits behind my stone shack on Stick Ross Mountain.

It is an early, chilly autumn and I am fighting my ceaseless battle against the frosty elements that penetrate my deteriorating plastic windows, seep through cracks between the stones where the mortar has fallen out, and radiate from the thin concrete pad that serves as my floor. The straw is long gone, disposed of when first a tarantula, and then a copperhead snake, pay me an uninvited visit. Earl and I split wood together, but the far superior tin wood stove he installed (the forty-dollar version) burns much less of it and puts out fantastic heat. Doesn't hurt that he has sealed up all the cracks in his cabin, repaired his windows, and covered the wood-plank floor with carpet scraps. I discover that this guy, visionary Aquarius that he is, who practices yoga, engages in radical politics, and enjoys the Moody Blues, is actually a super-practical fellow who can build or fix almost anything. I have not known such men. My dad, as my mom is fond of saying, needs supervision to change a light bulb. My boyfriends, and a first husband from a brief marriage, who was charming and talented and hopelessly addicted to almost everything, have all been musicians or singers or actors lacking in useful worldly skills. But Earl is a working class guy with solid rural roots who has picked cotton and grown gardens, taken apart cars and put them back together, built microwave ovens in a factory, been an air traffic controller, is an expert marksman (though he has foregone guns in the interest of building a peaceful world), can hunt and skin edible animals (though he is now a vegetarian), and can cook. Yeh, a guy that cooks. He teaches me how to slow cook strange foods like pinto beans and black-eyed peas on the woodstove until they are saucy and flavorful. I revel in such solid fare, and wave farewell to my fruitarian days.

There is one thing, however, that really seals the deal. Earl wants a family. Unheard of in these free-wheeling, free-loving, irresponsible days. He actually wants kids. With nary a look behind me, I eventually abandon my stone-cold shack and my twenty-dollar tin stove, and move ten feet away into his cozy little wood cabin. *A very, very, very fine house.* And in the decade to come, we do have kids, four of them, starting the very next year. Four very, very, very fine boys.

1 How We Ended Up in Paradise

EARL AND I WERE nomads through most of our first decade as a family, seeking an elusive combination of community, land, meaningful employment, and alternative schooling for our boys. Certain values were at the forefront of our thinking. Like so many of our generation, we wanted to live with a light ecological footprint, build ourselves a sustainable dwelling, grow our own food, and develop alternative sources of energy. We wanted to devote time to meditation and spiritual growth. We wanted to be part of a dynamic community of people who shared our values. Most of all, we wanted our children to experience the same freedom of exploration in their education that we had experienced in Flaming Rainbow. At times, we realized one or another of the components of the dream, but never all of them simultaneously. We might find the right community, but there was no school. Or we would find a great school—in an urban area. The right land, but no jobs, so no money to build a house.

We lived for awhile in the Huerfano Valley in southern Colorado, a remote and beautiful area populated with scores of communes and all the trappings of the counterculture—food coop, free clinic, lay midwives, experimental architecture, rock bands, poets, artists, and a charming little preschool. I was even able to indulge my show-business persona there, performing in the enormous dome that served as theater and community party hall. When Allen Ginsberg was slated to debut his new poem there, "Plutonium Ode," I choreographed a somber dance movement to the strains of Penderecki's "Threnody to The Victims of Hiroshima." Unfortunately,

Allen was ill, and couldn't make it down from Boulder, so poet and founding father of one of the big communes, Peter Rabbit, read it instead while I danced. Peter Rabbit was renown in the Huerfano for his poetry and his temper and his home-brewed Cottontail Ale (with the hip hops), a potent hallucinogenic brew that contained an ounce of strong marijuana bud leaf in each case of quart bottles.

A Rare Formal Portrait, circa 1984:
Steven, Chris, Shaman, Räm

It was a utopian experiment that called us in many ways...
except for the fact that we were parents, and unfortunately, in this
hippie/artist/existentialist haven, the kids pretty much ran wild
while the grown-ups carried on with their creative, hedonistic
lifestyles. Our idea of parenting included, in addition to monog-
amy, some ridiculously conventional things like regular meals,
warm jackets, and predictable bedtimes. I had forgiven Diego, my
son's little preschool friend, for getting him intoxicated on beer
at the annual Hog Farm baseball game in New Mexico, but my
guts truly clenched when one day, walking down to the communal garden to pull weeds, I came across a group of children, the
oldest perhaps eight, smoking weed and drinking whiskey from
a small flask. My dreams and Earl's common sense instructed us
in unequivocal terms to move on, which turned out to be a wise
move. A few months later, most everyone in the Valley, including
Peter Rabbit, was rounded up in a huge raid, complete with black
helicopters, for growing and selling marijuana.

We seemed trapped in impossible contradictions: to have jobs
that supplied the resources to develop our dream lifestyle meant
not having the time to develop our dream lifestyle. Or we'd have
the time, but no money. In hindsight, our dreams outdistanced any
capacity we had to realize them. One scheme that looked prom-
ising was an invitation to Earl to travel to Columbia to purchase
emeralds with a small group of hippie investors, and he was enough
of an adventurer to go for it. Our reasoning went something like
this: a few trips down there, we double or triple our investment,
buy a nice big piece of land, and start down the path towards
self-sufficiency. There were a few glitches we didn't anticipate. One,
that the emerald trade in Columbia was like the wild west of the
California Gold Rush—the domain of gangsters, paramilitaries,
drug lords, and a chain of dealers ranging from the reputable to
the criminal. Another, that the Bogota police would not hesitate to
drag long-haired *turistas* into alleys, jab guns in their backs, and
strip search them. Or that potential thieves would follow them

to their hotel and accost them with knives. All of which actually happened. Less dangerous, but equally devastating was the very real possibility of spending the stake we had painstakingly accumulated on a dazzling green fake.

In a Small Town Near Paradise

The Goddess of Dumb Luck smiled upon us, however, and the hero overcame these obstacles to return home safely with a pouch full of the most magnificent, sparkly green stones imaginable. We were set to rock and roll. To our dismay, we discovered that no jeweler in his right mind would buy expensive emeralds from a long-haired guy in jeans. The short version of this story is that Earl, who proved to be surprisingly attuned to the subtle qualities of expensive rocks, became a legitimate gem wholesaler, with a short haircut and a suit, and a sales route that covered multiple states. For years, he left the house like any other traveling salesman, albeit one with a half-million dollars worth of stones in his shoulder bag on any given day. From this description, you might think we actually got rich, but the truth was, we had fallen into a business that was not only extraordinarily expensive to run, with all the travel expenses and the cost of registering every package that went out, but also required substantial infusions of cash into its operating capital to replenish inventory. So, we did not really solve the problem of having enough disposable income. And we did not solve the problem of free time either, coming late to the realization that having your own business meant working twice as much as having a job. But it did address one of the variables in our lifestyle equation: location. An independent traveling salesman could live just about anywhere as long as there was a highway nearby.

So we moved to the outskirts of a tiny town high in the Sangre de Christo mountains of Northern New Mexico. No longer a total vegetarian, Earl was enticed by the trout fishing in the Cimarron River (estimated four thousand catchable-sized wild browns per mile, for those of you who are interested in such things), and I was enticed by the breathtaking views of the surrounding national forest and romantic notions of the contemplative life—with two young children and a third on the way. As anyone with any sense could have told us, it was an utterly impractical move for a number of reasons. Earl was gone for days at a time traveling around the Southwest in our one vehicle, a 1976 white Ford F150 Supercab pick-up truck, selling gemstones. I stayed home in our mountain retreat with five-year-old Shiva Kumar and one-and-a-half-year-old Shaman Blue Sky.

Grace Slick of the Jefferson Airplane, my favorite female rock star at the time, considered naming her child "god" with a small g, but she and Paul Kantner had a change of heart and named her China instead. That doesn't excuse Earl and me, but it does place us firmly in a context of counterculture parents breezily naming their children after ancient gods and goddesses and a variety of animals, vegetables, minerals, weather, and states of consciousness. Shiva Kumar was christened by an orange-turbaned Indian monk and Shaman—well, before he was born, he visited me in a dream and told me his name. I trusted my dreams pretty unconditionally, having immersed myself in them with Uncle River, my Jungian psychoanalyst buddy from my Flaming Rainbow days. Perhaps this one might not have influenced me so profoundly had Shaman not been born the spitting image of his dream self.

Just to get to the post office required a one-mile trek along a two-lane mountain road. I was hugely pregnant, and with Shaman in a blue corduroy Snugli on my back, I probably looked to people driving by like a lumbering hippo on the road. But hardly anyone ever drove by. The nearest grocery store that carried what I considered edible food was the Taos Coop, a forty-five-minute drive down an awesomely beautiful canyon. I navigated that treacherous winding road with Shiva Kumar, Shaman Blue Sky, and the as-yet-unnamed-and-unborn-one every other week or so when Earl and the Ford came home, to stock up on organic provisions and get a glimpse of other humans.

Despite the challenges and the isolation, the boys and I were having a grand time the summer that we moved there. We took long walks in the pine forest and Shiva Kumar and I made spontaneous haiku out of words that floated into our minds.

Breeze blows in our ears
soft feeling under our feet
I hear the river.

Haiku, by the way, is a great way to learn about syllables.

Steve's First Day of School, New Mexico, 1978

We planted a little garden that produced lush vegetables, due, I suspect, to its location atop the septic tank. We made fairy-tale puppets with papier-mâché heads, and an entire collection of Victorian Christmas tree ornaments out of thread spools, velvet, and odds and ends of beads and sequins. I knitted sweaters of rough wool to keep the boys warm in the coming winter, which turned out to be a doozy. Being philosophically opposed to the use of plastic, I also knitted woolen diaper covers for Shaman and his forthcoming brother, whose gender we did not know at the time, as I was also philosophically opposed to medical interventions like ultrasound. Nowadays, upscale parents who are philosophically opposed to plastic can purchase organic woolen tush protectors for around forty dollars, but at that time, if you wanted your baby's bum to breathe you knitted them yourself.

Just the Two of Us

The short mountain summer too soon turned to autumn, and the cool temperatures forced us into decision-making mode about Shiva Kumar's education. The closest school was at least a half hour away down the mountain, and I didn't see any compelling reason to interrupt all the good learning that was going on, but when I discovered that the kindergarten teacher lived next door (which in those parts meant "down the road a ways") and wouldn't mind driving him each day, I reluctantly enrolled the kid in school. Why not? After all, kindergarten was only a half-day, he could make some little friends, and we could still do haiku in the afternoons. Foreshadowing his uncanny ability to adapt to mainstream culture, Shiva Kumar took control of his destiny, demanded a haircut, changed his name to Steve, and got set to join the world of the schooled.

I'm going to give her the benefit of the doubt and say that perhaps this teacher had the best interests of her kindergarten students in mind, but when Steve told me that the very first thing they had done in school was to get a good look at the long wooden paddle hanging on the wall by her desk and hear all the potential sins that might induce her to use it on them, I went ballistic.

"The first day of school in their whole lives and this is how you get started?" I asked in an uncharacteristically shrill voice when she dropped him off the next day. "A paddle! What are you thinking?"

I didn't pull him out of school with righteous indignation—at the time, I didn't perceive that we had many viable options—but I made it very clear to his teacher that there would be dire consequences if she so much as laid an unfriendly hand on my child. Probably not the best approach to cultivating neighborly relationships, but I had discovered my inner lioness. Corporal punishment was not in our repertoire of behavior-management strategies, which was surprising, considering the fact that Earl was regularly "whupped," at home and at school in the Oklahoma of the 1950's. He's living proof that you *can* change those nasty patterns. This experience was perhaps the first inkling I had that our dream of living in a remote rural area might be incompatible with other fantasies, such as living our progressive ideals in a community of like-minded souls. I think that paddle sowed the seeds of my unrest about public schooling. But these would take some time to germinate.

A few years later, we were living in a small university town in north-central Oklahoma, where the Colorado gem company that Earl now worked for had transferred him to open up a new sales territory. Steve had begun fourth grade as a new student at a brand-spanking-new suburban school around the corner from our brand-spanking-new rented tract house on Brooke Avenue. The school was so new that it sat atop an unsightly mound of naked red Oklahoma dirt, which to my chagrin had been a landfill in the not-too-distant past. Shaman had begun his school career in a super-large kindergarten class at the same school. I was a stay-at-home mom with three-year-old Räm and yet another baby boy, Christopher.

I worked very hard at being a model public school parent at the new suburban school. I volunteered for everything and visited my children's classrooms to do art projects, tell stories wearing funny hats, and present puppet shows. I'm sure Steve was especially thrilled when I came to his class to demonstrate the wonders of cooking with whole grains and legumes. Though we were living in the middle of soybean-producing country, none of the local kids had ever eaten one. I made cookies with his classmates chock full of wheat germ, sunflower seeds, nutritional yeast, and blackstrap molasses in a largely unsuccessful effort to steer them away from their Twinkies. To my No. 1 Son's credit, he has never expressed resentment for my meddling, despite embarrassing lunchboxes packed with tofu and alfalfa sprouts, and what I insisted *was* Kool-Aid in his thermos (bright red hibiscus and rose hips tea sweetened with honey).

I suppose my effort to change the eating habits of Steve's school friends was one expression of my ambivalence about having the boys in public school. Except for the fact that it rested on a landfill, our new suburban school was not a horrible place. The building was clean, it had many resources, nice playgrounds, and the teachers all worked very hard at what they did. But given the enormous cultural tsunami that hit shore in the sixties and rolled through seventies, our countercultural leanings, and our youthful impatience, there were irreconcilable differences between what we wanted for our kids and what the school was prepared to offer.

It's difficult to pinpoint exactly when Earl and I decided we could do a reasonably good job of educating our four sons, but a defining moment occurred on a visit to Shaman's kindergarten class. Lois, a gentle, soft-spoken young teacher, seemed slightly overwhelmed by the forty-four five-year olds in her care, with only an assistant teacher to help with crowd control. She had called me in for the dreaded parent conference, and in her sweetly diplomatic way, suggested that Shaman was causing her just the slightest bit of trouble.

Lois: He's a wonderful boy. And he's extremely bright.

Me: Yes....? *(waiting, breath drawn, for the "but")*

Lois: You know, we've been doing a unit on dinosaurs. I've done a lot of work to prepare the unit.

Me: *(eagerly)* Shaman LOVES dinosaurs. He reads constantly about dinosaurs, and has been writing and illustrating little books about them. Right now, he is constructing a huge papier-mâché brontosaurus at home.

Lois: Well, that's what I wanted to talk to you about. It's just a little bit embarrassing when he corrects my pronunciation of dinosaur names, or when he tells me, in front of the class, that my information is outdated. Perhaps you could talk to him.

Startled, I wasn't sure how to respond. Okay, it probably was embarrassing to be corrected by a five-year-old, but couldn't a teacher appreciate having a kid with a lot of information to share in the classroom? Mightn't she capitalize on this rather than feeling threatened by it? Trying to figure out a way to broach the subject with Shaman, I wandered over to the learning center where he was engaged in an activity that involved green construction paper, dried kernels of corn, and Elmer's glue. He had been patiently gluing the kernels of corn onto a capital E for the past fifteen minutes and was about a quarter of the way through. An agreeable child, he sighed, and said, "This is boring," but continued to work on it. I cornered Lois after school to ask the purpose of the corn-gluing activity.

"It's a hands-on way to learn their letters," Lois said patiently.

"I figured that. But he already knows his letters," I said. "Actually, he knows how to read. And write. Remember those dinosaur books I told you about?"

"Each child needs to cycle through the alphabet learning center to make the letters."

"You mean HE IS GOING TO HAVE TO GLUE CORN ON ALL 26 LETTERS? At this rate, it will take him the whole year! Why not let him sit over in the book corner and read dinosaur books instead? It seems like a waste of time to glue corn onto letters if he already knows how to read."

"We couldn't do that," said Lois. "If he didn't do the activity, the other children might not want to do the activity. *We can't let one child do something different.*"

There you have it. The seeds of my unrest were sprouting.

Next year, in the summer of 1983, we bought a piece of land for $675 an acre, eight miles outside of town on dirt roads in the historic Paradise Township, in Paradise Valley. Nourished by the utopian visions of Helen and Scott Nearing, the Shakers, and the *Mother Earth News*, we aimed to do our part in the imminent revolutionary transformation of our consumer society by living a life of ecological sustainability and voluntary simplicity. Originally, our twenty acres was hunting grounds for Pawnee, Cheyenne, Arapaho, Osage, Quapaw, and Kaw, until the passage of the Federal Homestead Act of 1862 opened up the land for white settlement. The infamous Oklahoma Land Run of 1889 *accelerated* the revolutionary transformation of the North American continent *away from* ecological sustainability and voluntary simplicity (think "Big Oil"). Our deed to the property originated with the first white settler who got his acreage for free in that vast land grab from the natives. The crumbling stone foundation and caved-in well from that settlement were still visible—as was a rusty old whiskey still in a grove of cedar trees. Bootlegging was undoubtedly more profitable than trying to eke out a living growing crops on the stubborn red clay soil.

Digging the Well

That summer, an elderly, grizzled fellow in a battered red pick-up truck came with a Y-shaped stick and dowsed the property in a mysteriously successful attempt to locate a deep and pure spring of water. He dug us a well for the unbelievable (today) price of two hundred dollars. Earl somehow managed to find us an old 984-square-foot wooden house for sale up in Pawnee, which we transported to Paradise and set upon a new concrete foundation for the grand sum of two thousand dollars. It had never occurred to me that you could actually move a whole house, but Okies are remarkable for their abilities to reuse and recycle, always have been ever since the Dust Bowl rendered that place uninhabitable for all but the most hardy, resourceful, and adaptable humans. We rototilled a substantial garden plot, started a monster compost heap, and made the house reasonably habitable. *Reasonably* is the operative word here, but more about that later.

With the approach of autumn, yet another defining moment in our educational decision-making occurred. I paid a visit to the local rural school, in a town where the phone book contained disturbingly few surnames, and discovered that the school bus ride would be about an hour and a half each way for Steve and Shaman. Misgivings turned into serious reservations when I inquired into the curriculum and learned from the principal that literature and the arts were not included at this school because "all of these kids are going to end up on tractors anyway."

Well, I thought. Three hours a day on dusty old back roads on a school bus, to a school that doesn't value music, art, dance, or drama. Not to mention haiku.

This would never do.
We were in a quandary.
Perplexed and confused.

We yearned to be modern homesteaders, experimenting with self-sufficiency and trying to live our lives with a small ecological footprint. But once again, our values and dreams clearly were not in sync with the dominant ones in the local township. What to do?

We took stock of our situation. Coming of age in the sixties, we had lived our young adult lives rebelling against conventional ways of doing things. Our experience in Flaming Rainbow had taught us that we could learn and do anything we put our minds to. We had educated ourselves about natural childbirth and delivered two of our kids by ourselves. We had grown successful gardens and had already built one house (well, half a house). We had evolved from the *turn on, tune in, drop out* generation into the *use it up, wear it out, make it do, or do without* sector of society. We—not just our little family, but a whole generation of experimentalists—had become a subculture valiantly striving to create an alternate world free of greedy corporations, crooked politicians, and authoritarian dictums of all kinds. We had educated ourselves about war, consumerism, the destruction of the environment, and a host of other ills, and many of us saw our own formal educations as implicated in the mess our society had become. Why not try our hand at schooling—or *unschooling*—our own children?

We decided that there was a vast amount of useful knowledge to be gained from the modern homesteading experience. The boys could learn to grow food, raise animals, build things, study nature, and read to their heart's content. We could make a mini-Flaming Rainbow! I worried that we might get arrested for not sending our children to school, so I spent some time in the local university library researching the education laws in Oklahoma. Happily, I discovered that the existence of scores of unaccredited Christian schools in this largely rural state, coupled with the very real political power of the fundamentalists, created a cozy context of extremely loose laws governing children's education. If one *were* to get into trouble for not sending one's offspring to school, it would only be necessary to demonstrate that we were providing an "equivalent" education to what might be offered in the government-run schools. Given my instructive meeting with the rural school principal, I figured the burden of proof was well within our capacity. So we spent the next five years unschooling in Paradise, and just in case the authorities came to haul us away, I typed up the details of what we did each day on an old manual typewriter so that I might wow the judge with impressive arguments for our educational arrangements, should that opportunity arise.

The saga begins
An experiment is launched
Unschooling unfolds

First Christmas in Paradise, circa 1983

2 Tarantulas in the Freezer

IN EUROPEAN MEDIEVAL AND Renaissance paintings, Paradise is portrayed as a lush place where humans lounge contentedly in soft grass with their arms draped around lions and lambs. In my Romantic fantasies about living close to the land, I imagine walking barefoot in the early morning dew, lying out under the stars at night, wading in sparkling streams, and drinking tea in the shade of willow trees on summer afternoons. The Jane Austen version of a relationship with nature.

Our actual paradise was inhabited by scorpions, ticks, chiggers, brown recluse spiders and copperhead snakes, so walking barefoot at any time, let alone lying in the grass, was more or less precluded. Quiet nights under the stars were likely to be interrupted by howling coyotes. The closest body of water was a murky brown pond and standing on its shore one day, we all saw a water moccasin, sometimes called a "cottonmouth viper," swimming around in it, even though the university herpetologist we consulted was quite certain their habitat did not extend this far west. Their range line *was* supposedly just a few miles over, however, in Creek County, and we saw what we saw—long gray-green body slithering along the top of the water and that telltale fuzzy white mouth yawning open to reveal venomous fangs. Gives me the creeps even now just to think about it. Earl had stories to curl your hair about kids getting bitten to death by swarms of those nasty reptiles even in the bigger Oklahoma lakes. Rural legends? At any rate, I ruled out pond swimming, if not lake swimming, and I never did find a clear sparkling stream anywhere in Oklahoma to wade in. To top off the demise of my

Romantic notions, Oklahoma summers are too bloody hot even in the shade to enjoy afternoon tea.

In the best of worlds, one's dwelling offers respite from the dangers and discomforts of the great outdoors. However, the boundaries between inside and outside are permeable when you live in a construction site, and seeing that our recycled house was basically a work-in-progress the whole time we lived there, we were continuously invaded by a variety of noxious creatures. Science fiction writers and doomsayers predict that after we have fully wreaked our ecological havoc on the planet, the world will be taken over by insects. I fully support their theory. In fact, our little spot on Gaia was living proof of the ingenuity, persistence, and general evolutionary superiority of our multilegged planetary partners. If you are at all squeamish about things that bite, sting, pinch, burrow, creep, itch, or blister, or if you want to hang onto Romantic notions about your relationship with nature, you might want to skip this chapter.

The positive side of living a participatory existence within an ecosystem swarming with life is that your science classroom is right at hand. The negative side of living a participatory existence within an ecosystem swarming with life is that your living room is the laboratory. Our investigatory tools were simple: a high-intensity lamp, X-Acto blades, measuring tape and rulers, kitchen knives, magnifying glass, jewelry pliers, flat Styrofoam cartons, jars, and the freezer. And we didn't even have to go out the front door for our specimens.

One of our earliest exciting discoveries occurred one summer day when we noticed a large clump of dried red mud near the ceiling. A wasp was flying in and out of the mud clump, so we invoked the inductive scientific method to hypothesize that it might be a wasp's nest. We waited patiently for a moment when there were no wasps around—poor Steve had already experienced the wasp defense mechanism—and then scraped the dried red clay blob off the wall with a putty knife. With great anticipation—this really was exciting, but perhaps you had to be there—we carefully sliced it open, hoping to get a good cross-section view. We discovered an architectural marvel consisting of a cluster of short parallel tubes, covered over with a layer of mud like a New Mexico adobe house. To our surprise, a mass of itsy bitsy white spiders swarmed about. Spiders? We were expecting to see wasp larvae.

Further exploration into one of the many mud tubes did yield a squirming white larvae in a transparent egg case and an *Aha!* moment occurred when we realized that the baby spiders must be its food, flown in by the conscientious mother. Upon further research in the trusty World Book, we discovered that this solitary creature (unlike others of their species they are not social and do not live in colonies) was actually doing us untold favors by hunting, stinging, and paralyzing spiders, usually black widows, packing them into the mud tunnels with her head, and laying eggs upon the not-yet-dead spiders before sealing up the tunnel. One of the unfortunate spiders must have been carrying an egg sack. Mystery solved. But we were faced with a problem of both ecological and aesthetic dimensions. Should we allow our guest to continue her reproductive labors in our house, ridding us of countless dangerous spiders? Or would it just be too much to keep a mud dauber's nest in a prominent corner of the living room? Aesthetics won the day, and the patched up nest, some extra mud, and the baby spiders were put in a gallon glass jar on the porch, while Steve and Shaman commenced to record their observations.

Another group of creatures that provided endless opportunities for study were the red fire ants. Incredibly industrious, these creatures create impressive underground networks of tunnels and chambers to store their food. After a rainfall, they clear debris from their doorways and halls, creating conspicuous mounds of red dirt, a bit like those made by gophers. One evening, Shaman intervened in the normal cycle of nature, filling a plastic bucket with dirt and depositing a fair number of the population of a red ant colony into it. The next morning, he was thrilled to find that they had burrowed into the dirt overnight. He continued to restock the artificial colony, taking special note of how far up the sides the ants could climb before they fell, and seeing if it made a difference when he rubbed sand or water on the inside of the bucket. That's called "changing your independent variable" in science talk, which hints that kids might well be hardwired for the scientific method if we let them go about their business. Further explorations included activities like spreading grains of sugar in patterns to watch the red ant troops follow the leader. Once we all found a tarantula lying by a fire ant hole with ants swarming around it. We wondered how it died. Could the ants, collectively, have killed such a disproportionately large creature? We watched the food orgy until our attention was diverted by mating grass-hoppers. How exciting can life be?

It's one thing to come upon a dead tarantula outside, where it belongs, and quite another to have a live one in your kitchen. Despite my initiation into the world of arachnids at Stick Ross Mountain, I never quite came to terms with sharing my living space with them, and here was one of those creatures with its long hairy legs and bulbous body hopping merrily about while I stirred the beans on the stove. I did not know at the time that tarantulas are mostly nonaggressive toward humans or that their bite is comparable to a mere wasp or bee sting. Absent such reassuring knowledge, I found these creatures mildly terrifying. What to do with a tarantula in the kitchen? I certainly didn't want to smash it because then I would have to clean it up. Besides, we were trying to model a sense of "deep ecology" for our kids that went something like this: *We all share this tiny planet, and every living creature has inherent worth, and just as much of a right to be here as we do. Therefore, we should not take any life unnecessarily.* Despite the commitment to species rights, I did not believe that every crea-ture had a right to find its way into someone's bedroom slippers. Even though I had trained the boys early on in our homesteading adventure to shake everything out before putting it on, I lived in dread of nasty critters lurking in underwear drawers, bed sheets, or shoes. I wanted that hairy monster out of my house. A corollary to our evolving philosophy, derived from idealized Indian lore, was *if you have to take a life to satisfy vital needs, make use of every scrap of it.* So rights aside, maybe there was a way to make full use of it. I knew the boys would get a kick out of a close-up view of Monster Spider, and that my standing as Super Earth Mother would increase tremendously should I surprise them with such a magnificent specimen. That's where the freezer comes in.

Where the Wild Things Are, circa 1983
Steven, Shaman, Räm, Chris

When attempting to capture a creature with eight eyes, it's no easy task to situate yourself out of its range of vision. I did know that tarantulas could leap, but wasn't sure how far. I definitely did not want it to leap on me. So I snuck up from the rear and clamped a Mason jar down over it, creating an instant terrarium. Voilà! Safely encased in glass. Now came the scary part, when I had to quickly turn the damn thing over and clamp a lid on it. Gazing deep into its eight eyes, I communicated my apologies and stuck it in the deep freeze, so that later, the boys might be able to study those hairy legs and little claws and venomous fangs really close up.

Presumably tarantulas, being cold-blooded creatures who regularly experience the deep freeze of winter, do not experience pain or discomfort from this sort of slow, cold death. I want to believe this, but in fact, I really don't know, and I admit to some minor moral qualms about such "interventions" we undertook in the name of science—everything from spray painting gorgeous new morning spider webs with white spray paint and lifting them carefully onto black construction paper to occasionally freezing insects and butterflies for mounting and closer inspection. Ethical dilemmas arose: What does "deep ecology" really infer? What are "vital needs" and who should decide this? How far need our sympathies extend? Should we interfere in the course of nature in the service of constructing knowledge? What does it matter, in the bigger picture, if Spider Mom has to spin a new web in order to capture a meal? After all, there's a good chance that she will be paralyzed and stuffed into an earthen tube by Wasp Mom before lunch. Or if fire ants find themselves inexplicably hemmed in by plastic walls? What does it mean to have a "relationship with nature," when nature is not a nineteenth-century English countryside, but a harsh, hot, and threatening ecosystem populated by venomous creatures? And perhaps, most important, how can we make these questions part of the "curriculum?"

Cocker spaniels and butterflies are easy to love. But respect for nonhuman species has to include those creatures that are downright hostile to humans and ugly to boot. In fact, some of the nastiest, lowliest creatures may be the most crucial to the maintenance of ecosystems. How can we learn to appreciate these underappreciated species if we don't take the time to carefully observe their marvelous engineering feats, their superb defense mechanisms, their incalculable contributions to ecological balance (think spiders and flies), and the stunning designs that have evolved in response to the environment (eight eyes—wow!)?

Few kids in the United States today have the opportunity to study nature up close and personal. Farm families are forced off the land to make way for industrialized food production. Our wild spaces are disappearing, given over to suburbs, condos, and malls. Where there *are* spaces to wander in, many parents are too fearful—of dirt and germs and accidents and predators—to let the kids loose. Lives are too highly scheduled and structured to make time for wandering and exploration. But how does one develop an appreciation for the natural world without spending a significant amount of time in it? If we're going to love the earth and its creatures enough to save it, we need to really love it, not some Romantic ideal of nature or an intellectual abstraction of it, but the real deal, in all its teeming, hairy, ugly, creepy, crawly, slithering, slimy, swarming, buzzing, biting, sucking, stinging glory. If we can learn to love the wasps and the scorpions and the red ants and the tarantulas, there is hope for the planet. Besides, they outnumber us. And they may outlast us. For that alone, they deserve our respect.

3 Our House...

Such a cozy room, the windows are illuminated by the
Sunshine through them, fiery gems for you, only for you.
~Crosby, Stills, Nash and Young

To this day, I am haunted by dreams of unfinished houses. Sometimes the house is on Stick Ross Mountain. Sometimes it is in Paradise Valley. It may be in the hills of Vermont or on the edge of a rocky precipice in Tibet. The recurring dream house takes many forms—it has appeared as a multistory affair with massive unfurnished rooms, and as a compact structure built into a dank cave, like the house we once bought in Evergreen, Colorado, where Chris was born. I've dreamt of houses made of adobe, like the ones I fell in love with in New Mexico, and of wood and stone. But no matter the shape or the materials, the house is always incomplete.

In most dreams, some or all of the boys are there, usually as youngsters, but sometimes as their adult selves. Occasionally Earl shows up. I'm not sure what these recurring house dreams are all about. Unfinished business I suppose, my psyche's laborious journey toward wholeness. Perhaps they just represent regret at never having been able to provide my kids with the house I envisioned for them. The house with shining wood floors and rag rugs for cozy lounging in front of fireplaces. Wall shelves bulging with books and board games. Bedrooms for everyone, handmade quilts on the beds. Pots and pans hanging above the stove in the kitchen, hot loaves of fresh-baked bread and a wooden bowl of just-picked apples on a big plank table, just like in those country-living magazines. A root cellar with boxes of sand filled with harvested carrots and potatoes, and jars of preserved jams and tomatoes and chutneys lining the walls. An herb garden right outside the kitchen door. A hippie version of Martha Stewart. My mother always bemoaned the fact that "when you're young, you can never afford the house you need; when you get old and can afford it, you don't need it anymore." In this, as in other things, she was right on. But my mother did have a functional, if not fancy, three-bedroom ranch in the suburbs by the time her only child started school. I, on the other hand, had four kids in a construction site.

Being nomads of the hippie generation, we had occupied a crazy quilt of shelters. The best was probably the house in Tahlequah where Steve was born, a gleaming white, wood two-story that looked gorgeous from the outside, but which had been abandoned by divorcing owners in the middle of a remodeling job. We lived in the habitable rooms and kept the doors closed on the ones that had been gutted.

We had tried homesteading once before in Paradise Valley, just a couple of section roads over, when Steve was a toddler and an only child. We had friends who had bought land and built houses there, and when Earl got offered a carpentry job in the area, we jumped at the chance to do so ourselves. That adventure had us living in an army tent for sixteen months. When the Oklahoma monsoons came, Earl had to dig a hasty moat around the tent to keep the floodwaters out, but at least there were no spring tornadoes that year. In the summer, we suffocated in hundred-degree-plus heat and in the winter we woke with frost on our sleeping bags. I had to break the ice in the diaper bucket with an axe.

We bathed outside with a hose, year around, which undoubtedly made Steve the hardy creature he is today (we're talking about a man whose idea of a good time is cycling across the Norwegian plateau on a fixed-gear and bivouacking on rocks and snow). I cooked on an open fire until we bought a little kerosene camp stove. After that exploded and caught fire one day, I went back to the wood fire in a rock-lined pit. We heated the tent with a tin wood stove, which warmed us if we stayed within an eighteen-inch radius. Civilization advanced considerably when we finally ran a wire from the nearest Rural Electric pole to power a single hanging lightbulb, which made the place look like the interrogation quarters on a military outpost in Siberia. But it was home.

By the time I was pregnant with Shaman, Earl had managed to get us half a house built. The other half would have to wait until we saved more money for boards, so when winter approached, we nailed the tattered army tent over the gaping hole on the north side, which kept the worst of the howling wind and gusting rain at bay. The half house had a small but serviceable kitchen area with a functional water tap and a freezer, which worked fine until a rat chewed through the cord one night and got sizzled while we slept. By the time we discovered what happened, our carefully preserved garden produce from the summer was sadly sodden.

There was a living room space that was always filled with friends passing through during that post-sixties migratory drift. Not just friends; word spread in those Rainbow Trail days about places where you might rest your head and get a hot meal, and sometimes folks just showed up who were friends of friends of friends. Earl and I slept up in a loft atop Steve's bedroom, a space enclosed by studs, if not completed walls. The loft had a flat roof. One day one of those friends via six degrees of separation showed up with a backpack of peyote buttons that he had gathered down along the Rio Grande. The buttons needed drying, so he laid them out on that loft roof in the shape of a Medicine Wheel.

Unlike some of my peers, I was diligent about what I put into my body during those childbearing/breastfeeding years. No coffee, no occasional glass of wine. So I didn't consider taking even a small bite of a button. But what colorful, meaningful dreams I had sleeping under the peyote that night! The Medicine Wheel lasted until the middle of the night when one of those predictable Oklahoma winds came along and blew the buttons off the roof and around the yard. In the morning, we were awakened by the squawking of the chickens dashing madly about pecking at the peyote.

Shaman was conceived around that time. He turned out to be a ten-pounder, and swelled my belly so much that I eventually couldn't make it up the ladder to the loft, so Earl built us a platform out of plywood with a mattress in the living room. By the time he was born, we had been able to afford insulation, but not interior sheetrock, for the three existing outside walls. The padded panels were made of pink cotton candy fiber filling covered with brown paper and a picture of Geronimo in red paint, complete with headdress. Shaman stared at this repetitive art installation from his baby seat for the first few months of his life.

We sold that three-walled place in spring to another aspiring homesteader and set out on our odyssey to the Huerfano Valley, where we'd heard about the flourishing alternative community deep in the Southern Colorado range of the Sangre de Christo mountains. Earl found work there as a carpenter, building a trust-fund hippie's recording studio, and we lived first in our camper, then in a tent trailer, and later in a two-room adobe hut. For a while, the four of us called a tiny Airstream trailer home while Earl built someone else a cabin high in the mountains. Living in such cramped spaces with two small children really got old, not to mention cold, in the mountain winter. I was happy to land in the ramshackle but spacious rental house in New Mexico, the one with the lush little vegetable garden atop the septic tank and the pine forest where we walked and made haiku.

Once Earl got into the gem business, we moved a lot for his work, and though the houses were never quite big enough, they generally had four walls, running water, and heat. I have always been an inveterate nester, eager to settle in a new place with whatever art and artifacts and homemade quilts and embroidered pillows I could haul around with me. Being uprooted was a more or less natural state of my being. Having left home at fifteen for Hollywood and been on the road in traveling shows for years, I had learned to make every new dwelling a home with just the contents of a suitcase.

BP (Before Paradise) From left to right:
Kathleen, Chris, Shaman, Steven, Earl, Räm

By the time we lived on Brooke Street, near the school built on a landfill, we looked to all appearances quite civilized. A wealthy aunt and uncle of mine had passed away, and my mom shipped us their Duncan Phyfe tables and dusty rose-brocade living-room chairs. Add to this some fabulous Persian and Indian rugs obtained in a trade with a Bogota emerald dealer, and we cut a posh picture. We slept in a real bed for the first time in our married life, not just a mattress on the floor, and I had a well-tooled kitchen. It was not exactly the house of our dreams. From Earl's point of view, if you could see your neighbor's chimney smoke, the houses were too close together. On Brooke St., I could stand in the tiny backyard and look over the waist-high chain-link fence in three directions and see endless exact replicas of our house, about six feet between them. But after giving birth to four kids in sketchy circumstances, traveling around the country living in everything from our truck to a tipi, and flitting from one community to another, I was content to settle in and live the straight life for awhile.

Big Sky, Little House

We finished out the school year there, Steve in the fourth grade class with his Twinkie-eating friends and Shaman in the corn-gluing kindergarten (I think he made it to *M*). Then—it must have been the advent of spring—the homesteading fever hit again, with its delirious off-the-grid dreams of a weightless ecological footprint and a well-stocked root cellar. Earl was the Aquarian visionary; I was the feet-on-the-ground practical Virgo, but much as I would like to, I can't blame this move solely on him. I was game and we were young, and still idealistic. We'd been so busy raising children and surviving that we failed to notice that many of our counterculture peers were now busy building 401Ks, not sustainable communities.

But there we were on our twenty acres—garden tilled, well dug, and a four-room shack (I'd call it a cottage, but that makes it sound quaint and cute) perched atop a newly poured concrete perimeter wall surrounding a crawl space. I didn't actually know what a crawl space was, but I quickly learned it was a space where creatures that crawl get under your house and find their way into it—scorpions, spiders, and the ubiquitous copperheads. Those copperheads were my nemeses, vying with tornadoes for first place in the *what I dislike most about Oklahoma* contest. In those first weeks, when we were painting the dull walls in our bedroom a cheery white, I came into the room to see one of those black-and-brown-patterned creatures slithering up the wall. Fortunately, Earl was there that day and took a shovel to it. Just pinned it to the wall and pressed until its head separated from its body. That man had nerves of steel. Another time, on a day he wasn't there, I was sorting out the stack of paper that we accumulated in our educational supplies closet and encountered one that had made its nest in the brightly colored tissue paper that we used for collage. The damn thing crawled up my arm to my neck and somehow, though I should have been paralyzed with fear, I managed to toss it off, scream, grab a broom, and maneuver it out the front door. The worst time, the time I almost truly lost it, was the evening I came into the bathroom and saw one on the floor beside the tub where Shaman was innocently bathing with his yellow rubber ducky. I jumped up on the side of the tub, and it scurried out the way it came in, through a crack in the floor where Earl had been working on the plumbing. If I'd had any sense, I would have packed us up that night and moved back to town. But I was not about to be one of those wussy females who got scared off by a few creepy crawly creatures.

We swept and scrubbed and painted and caulked the old single-pane glass windows as well as we could. Still, the wind still blew right through the house, kind of like in those Dust Bowl-era photographs. The wooden floors were so old that they were way past the refinishing stage. Centuries of Oklahoma dirt had burrowed into the grain of the wood, and no matter how much

I mopped, those floors never got clean. Just ruined all the mops. Baby Chris was still crawling when we moved in, and although it didn't bother him a bit, I hated seeing his little onesies always covered in red dirt.

The first major order of business was to build a tile floor protector and backdrop for a really fancy wood stove, as there was no heating system. After that, we managed to get one thing at a time done as the cash became available: a kitchen ceiling I designed to look like a Log Cabin quilt square and some decorative Mexican tile around the old porcelain kitchen sink. Creative pockets of loveliness amid the stud walls and sheetrock. Soon we had a new vinyl floor in the kitchen, and a handmade wooden island that I could clamp my wheat grinder onto. I was, at that point, grinding the flour for the four loaves of bread we consumed weekly. *And* making the tofu from scratch, *and* culturing the weekly gallon of yogurt with raw milk from the nice German farmers down the road. We were serious about this weightless footprint.

Some home-schooling families go out of their way to replicate "school" in their homes. Books and websites speak of the importance of creating "well-organized instructional spaces" with stacking trays to keep children's work for parental review, rolling carts with school supplies, and neat display spaces for artwork. Some particularly disciplined homes even have desks in rows (and a flag to recite the pledge to every morning), but many seat their youngsters around a dining table, à la Norman Rockwell, for their studies. We did have two small closets for books and games and paper, one of which that copperhead chose for its nest. And we had lots of display space—sheet rock is great for thumbtacks and pushpins and isn't the slightest bit bothered by tape.

But no desks, and not even a real eating space. Since we didn't have a home office for the gem business, Earl laid claim to our old Sears dining table, which stayed covered in pink carbon-copy receipts and the miniature Ziplock bags and tiny folded papers that held the Brazilian emeralds and amethysts and tourmalines and topaz of our trade. In the center of this treasure sat a precise, antique balance scale to weigh the gold and the gems. Our boys had the most beautiful math manipulatives in the world, and their early exposure to geometry, geology, mineralogy, and optics included vocabulary words like carats and facets, refraction and reflection, inclusions and calibration. They learned weights and measures in millimeters and grams, estimating the sizes of rubies, then checking their guess with calipers, and weighing sapphires opposite tiny bronze gram weights on the balance scale. We made a Norman Rockwell tableau of our own: Mom, Dad, and the kids in a dusty shack on the windswept plains, clustered around a suitcase filled with jewels on their dining table.

If the house fell way short of my fantasies, the outdoors was splendid. People who have never been there think of Oklahoma as one big dry flat plain that regularly gets flattened even more by giant winds. They are partially right—the state is right smack in the middle of Tornado Alley and in midsummer the hot winds blew so hard that when I hung out the laundered sheets, the first one would be dry before I pinched the last clothespin. But the image of flat plains and blowing tumbleweeds is incorrect, except perhaps when describing the Oklahoma Panhandle in the far west. Paradise Valley nestles in the heart of a complex ecosystem with the Tallgrass Prairie to the north, the wooded foothills of the Ozark Mountains to the east, grasslands to the west, and the Arbuckle, Ouachita, and ancient Kiamichi mountain ranges to the south. Massive herds of American Bison once rumbled across the plains, until brought to the point of extinction by the cowboys. This home where the buffalo roamed has a raw, fierce beauty and I felt a powerful connection to the land, despite the venomous creatures and extreme weather events. I was happiest outside, laboring in the garden or trekking through the woods with the boys, identifying and collecting flora and fauna. I cultivated an impressive talent for creative visualization, daily transforming our squalid living quarters into the house of my dreams, and Earl was content because he couldn't see the smoke from any nearby chimneys. To this day, our family never really talks about "our house in Paradise Valley." When we refer to that time in our lives, we always say "when we lived on the land" as though we were tipi dwellers, following the herds.

Now, those skeletal remains, as well as the remnants of that first half-built Oklahoma house, are busy biodegrading, sinking back into the earth to feed a new generation of oak and cedar trees. Though the land thrives—tangled, scrubby, bountiful, teeming with wildlife and pulsing with ancient memories of pounding buffalo hooves, it's been invaded by a new conqueror—the frackers. What began with the Homestead Act of 1862 now finds its culmination in desperate attempts to extract every possible bit of fossil fuel from these lands, and parts of Oklahoma, including Paradise Valley, have become what scientists call "sacrifice zones"—land irreversibly ruined by capitalism, technology, and toxic waste. Though I recall our days in Paradise nostalgically, I am grateful not to have to bear firsthand witness to the latest ecological devastation.

Just as my dear mother predicted, I've finally reached the point where I own the house of my dreams. It's in the mountains of Vermont, about as far from the cultural and natural ecosystem of Oklahoma as you can get and still be within the boundaries of the United States. But, as she also predicted, it's too late, save for the wonderful, but occasional family gatherings that take place there. My boys are well off on their grown-up life journeys, with house narratives of their own. I still dream of incomplete houses. If Uncle River were around, he would ask me, in his Jungian way, what "house" means to me. Life, I would say. The construction of a life. Security, stability, safety. None of which I have ever experienced in great measure. Completion. To some psychoanalysts, a house under construction suggests growth, energy, development. Perhaps it's not such a bad thing that my dream houses are always incomplete.

4 Doing "Good Science": On the Virtues of Simply Messing About

Who made the grasshopper?
This grasshopper, I mean—
the one who has flung herself out of the grass,
the one who is eating sugar out of my hand,
who is moving her jaws back and forth instead of up and
down—
who is gazing around with her enormous and complicated
eyes.
Now she lifts her pale forearms and thoroughly washes her
face.
Now she snaps her wings open, and floats away.
                    ~From "The Summer Day" by Mary Oliver

IN JULY AND AUGUST in Oklahoma, countless millions of locusts and grasshoppers leap through gardens and fields, chomping their way through whatever hardy green leaves or stalks remain standing by that time. Lazy summer days bring the ubiquitous background hum of these creatures rubbing their ridged hind legs against their wings, an erotic song aimed at the properly attuned antenna of the opposite sex. To humans, especially those of the gardening variety, this insistent buzz resonates with ancient, archetypal dread. I have never actually seen a swarm of locusts, like you read about in the Bible, or which still occur regularly in parts of India and Africa, but given the damage that the southwestern variety can perpetrate, I can only imagine the mythic terror when the sky darkens and the unceasing drone amplifies like in a scene out of a Hitchcock movie.

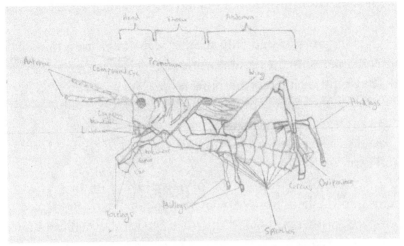

Papa's Grasshopper (by Revati, 2018)

Given the pervasive presence of these creatures on our homestead, it was not surprising that the boys would take an interest in their habits. One day in mid-August, I was struggling against the elements—late summer drought, scorching heat, and a host of invading insects, including the grasshoppers—to salvage something of our garden. As I weeded and mulched and relocated potato beetles from the potato plants to a can of kerosene, I noticed Shaman, who was eight years old at the time, sitting on our front stoop, gazing intently at something that he held in his fingers. From the garden I couldn't tell what it was. Forty-five minutes or so later, my curiosity piqued, I found an excuse to go into the house and stopped to visit with him. He was still sitting in the same position, holding a grasshopper by its hind legs and attempting to feed it a stem of grass.

"Hey, what's up?" (One of my top ten open-ended questions.)

"He was drowning in a puddle. I saved him."

"Hmmh. So what are you doing?" (Another of the top ten.)

"I'm trying to figure out how its jaws work," he replied, staring intently at the creature.

"Well, what have you found out?" (Yet another of the top ten.)

"It has lips and teeth and it spit out a brown juice when I picked it up."

"Eeooh, gross," I said (My surefire way of ensuring the boys' intense interest in the natural world.)

"But I still can't figure out how its jaws work."

"How 'bout you look it up in the *World Book*?" (Fallback position when I have no clue.)

And so, he headed indoors to find a jar for the captured critter and carry on his investigations.

After another hour or so of Sisyphean labor in the garden, I went into the house to see what was up. Shaman had created a ten-page grasshopper book with detailed pencil-drawn illustrations and relevant text, complete with a green-colored paper cover. I learned from reading this delightful little text that grasshoppers' mouths have two large, horny lips. I learned that between their lips is a pair of sharp jaws called mandibles and that behind the mandibles is another pair of jaws with feelers that taste and eat grass. I learned that they have five eyes. Five eyes! Wow! And what an amazing abdomen—eleven segments that work sort of like a telescope, expanding out so that the female can deposit her eggs deep in our Oklahoma soil. And those ovipositors—sharp things at her rear end powerful enough to dig holes in the ground! A truly amazing feat, given that I never found a shovel sharp enough to dig holes in the sun-baked red clay that passes for soil in central Oklahoma. Talk about adaptation.

Prior to this day, I mainly thought about grasshoppers, when I thought about them at all, as virulent enemies. Now, thanks to my son's diligent research and careful documentation, I had a new appreciation for the marvelous engineering of these hungry orthopterans. If the learning experience had ended here, it would have been a valuable one. Shaman had responded to something in his environment with interest and curiosity. He had utilized his powers of observation to develop further questions. When observations alone could not satisfy his curiosity, he went to printed source materials to find out what the experts had to say about the topic. And finally, he represented what he learned in a creative way that was both visually interesting and factually accurate. But this was only the beginning.

The next day I was again out in the garden fighting the good fight for my tomatoes, corn, and potatoes against everything that might burn, shrivel, or devour them before they reached our table. I noticed Shaman walking in ever-widening circles around the house. Periodically he would reach down into the tall grass that was forever encroaching and then walk back over to the stoop. Again, my curiosity got the best of me. I walked over to where he sat and noticed that he was marking a grasshopper with a black laundry pen.

"Did you know that grasshoppers can jump twenty times the length of their own body?" he asked as he leaped down from the stoop and let the creature loose.

"No I didn't," I responded. "How far could you jump if you could do that?"

He didn't take me up on that one, although I could see the wheels turn for a moment. Sometimes the best pedagogical questions simply do not resonate with what the learner has in mind. In this case, what he had in mind was collecting grasshoppers and marking them with the indelible pen. Hour after hour. As an art project, it wasn't up to his usual standards. I figured he must have some other, nonaesthetic motive. And indeed he did.

"What are you doing?"

"Marking the grasshoppers."

"I can see that."

Rolling his eyes back as if to say that anyone with any sense ought to know what he was up to, he patiently explained that he was marking the grasshoppers, releasing them, and then investigating in ever-widening concentric circles to see how far they were traveling from the house. He was interested in range, you see—an ecological concept that is not usually taught in primary school. As far as I recall, we had not talked about the concept. I would not have thought to build it into a "lesson plan." But here it was, emerging as an interest strong enough to justify devising a meaningful and systematic experiment. And systematic it was. For the next few days, Shaman continued to mark grasshoppers, to walk in circles around the house, and to search intently in the grass for the marked insects.

The results, as they say in the scientific world, were inconclusive. Given that we probably had a trillion or more of the creatures within a twenty-foot radius of the house, the chances of recapturing marked grasshoppers were slim at best. Surprisingly, he did find a couple. And the interest stayed with him long enough for us to have absorbing conversations about habitat, food chain, migration, range, and the procedures of investigative biological and ecological science.

I think of this story as an example of doing "good science," as opposed to "textbook science." Good science is messy and exploratory. Scientists operate on hunches that result from intensive study of a topic or problem. Experiments are designed based on these hunches. The outcomes of experiments are unpredictable. There are many dead ends. Textbook science, on the other hand, is tidy and predictable. All the facts are laid out in an orderly manner, as though one discovery had followed inevitably upon another. The scientific method is presented as a sort of unwavering sequence of hypothesis-experiment-evidence-results-conclusion. All of the chaos, confusion, and wrong turns are mostly absent from the textbook version of discoveries.

Many teachers do make heroic efforts to do "hands-on" or "discovery" science. Although there may be some manipulation of physical materials, there is seldom much actual discovery outside of what the teacher or textbook has in mind. Hands-on classroom activities are carefully structured, and designed primarily to teach students how to follow directions. They promote a number of procedural skills: observation, hypothesis formation, prediction, and the recording of data. A primary-school teacher might gather twenty-five Styrofoam cups and some potting soil, and provide the kids with instructions for planting, watering, and observing their seeds. Given the fact that many kids nowadays have never set foot in a garden, there is likely to be some excitement over this. They might measure the sprouts and record the growth on graphs, thus introducing an important math skill. But what are the chances on any given day that twenty-five first- or second-graders are all going to develop a passionate interest in the rate of growth of bean seeds? The excitement is likely to wane as each student, daily, is compelled to find time in between the Do Now, the spelling test, and the reading journals to dutifully record the minute growth of their bean plant.

In contemporary classrooms, there is little opportunity to engage in the exploratory processes that involve conceptualizing problems and planning experiments. And planning investigations is one of the most important and most neglected aspects of science learning. Planning is an imaginative activity that encourages children to think through the potential consequences of their actions. But it is time-consuming. To be more *efficient* (a major goal of factory education—as though learning was akin to making widgets), instructions for science activities are carefully delineated on instruction sheets or work cards in learning centers. Providing a set of instructions to follow effectively prevents children from engaging in planning. This approach to science, although better than no science at all, holds little promise of nurturing the "scientist within," for there is little scope for personal interest, extended observation, musing, the twists and turns of genuine exploration, or following a quest until the passion has been exhausted. The structure of the learning is external to the learner, the discovery process already laid out by adults who have predetermined the cognitive outcomes.

Shaman's grasshopper curriculum, on the other hand, while not structured by a lesson plan, was definitely not *unstructured*. In fact, there was a *deep structure* to the activity. First, there was an extended period of observation, in which he systematically noticed the intricate design details of the grasshopper. While doing this, a baffling question arose: *how do its jaws work?* Out of all the possible wonderings one might come up with, this was the one that intrigued him. This question structured both the observations and the subsequent investigations in the *World Book*. What he learned in the encyclopedia answered his initial question, but he had a need to reinforce his knowledge by generating a series of detailed drawings—of the mandibles, the digestive system, the limbs, and the reproductive system of this meticulously studied creature. He was not given an assignment to draw the various components of the grasshopper, he needed to draw them in order to internalize what he had learned, to make sense of things. And in this *making sense of*, this process of ordering his new knowledge conceptually, a new question arose: *if these creatures can hop twenty times the length of their bodies, how far from the house might they venture?* This new question then structured the next phase of the investigations—a planned experiment to discover the range of the grasshopper's habitat. The structure of the activity was inherent in the activity itself. The outcomes of the learning were not predetermined, nor was the direction of the study preplanned. It unfolded each step of the way.

It's not that grown-ups don't have an important role to play in learning. My guidance in this case was minimal— some casual questions, a suggestion to turn to a book for further knowledge, and then genuine interest in his creative product, from which I learned things that I did not know. But as his investigations reached a natural conclusion, I took a more active role and introduced new concepts—habitat, range, food chain, and migration—which built upon other experiences we had shared and which had the potential to lead to other, related areas of study. The concepts also named what he had learned, or provided theories for his experience. He had intuited the notion of range as he walked his concentric circles to see how far the grasshoppers roamed, but the theory that animals in an ecosystem have a normal range of movement is organized knowledge—knowledge that other scientific investigators have discovered through collective study. Not all knowledge can be, or needs to be discovered by the learner. But if knowledge is to be meaningful, if it is to result in significant cognitive change in a learner, it must connect with deeply felt interests, or needs, or questions. And these questions should, ideally, result from the interactions of a child with his or her material environment.

I am intrigued with the idea of "messing about," free and unguided exploratory work with concrete materials during which children test, probe, and experiment without imposed questions or instructions. Time for the unrestricted encounter with *stuff*, in which a child has the opportunity to touch, taste, feel, see, smell, manipulate, and experiment with the substances and elements, the objects and creatures, of the world. Such opportunities are all too circumscribed in formal school, a place in which now, more than ever, every moment is planned, premeditated, even scripted. Messing about is crucial to the beginnings of things, for it can foster curiosity, guesses, estimations, and speculations. Messing about raises questions that require further investigations. Messing about can necessitate the acquisition of new skills (measuring, using tools, doing calculations, handling substances).

Important as it is, of course, learning does not end with messing about. Guidance is essential, as is knowledge that has been discovered, organized, and synthesized by knowledgeable others. But to neglect the initial phases of observation, free play, creative thinking, and wondering, is to miss the opportunity to spark the thirst for inquiry that characterizes genuinely "good science."

5 The Hidden Curriculum of Schooling

I've noticed a fascinating phenomenon in my thirty years of teaching: schools and schooling are increasingly irrelevant to the great enterprises of the planet. No one believes anymore that scientists are trained in science classes or politicians in civics classes or poets in English classes. The truth is that schools don't really teach anything except how to obey orders.

~ From Dumbing Us Down, by John Taylor Gatto

MOST PARENTS WOULD AGREE that they want their children to enjoy learning and become independent thinkers, self-reliant workers, and creative problem-solvers. Solid middle-class American values, right? Such wonderful attributes are even found in many schools' mission statements. And yet most schools seem designed to achieve the opposite outcomes.

Shaman, being relatively unsocialized into the formal schooling experience, jumped right into self-directed learning on the order of the grasshopper experiments. Steve, however, had spent half a decade learning how to be a "good student," and in the beginning, seemed at loose ends. He asked me for assignments. I replied that we weren't doing this just so that I could give him assignments. I read John Holt's book *Teach Your Own* shortly after we began our unschooling adventure. Holt made a point in his book about what some folks call "debriefing" or "deprogramming" or even "detoxifying"— that it would likely take a child who had been in school an equivalent number of years to become self-directed in their learning when they began unschooling. It unnerved me, seeing as how, according to this theory, it could take Steve four years to become a self-directed learner. I didn't know if I could last that long.

I began to understand that schooled children assimilate a number of ideas that are essential to their educational success. First, they learn that knowledge needs to be dispensed by an authority figure in prescribed doses. They learn that there are right answers and wrong answers, correct and incorrect ways to think about things. They learn that other people are best suited to assign them work that proves they know these correct ways of thinking. They learn that what they are interested in is subordinate to state standards and grade-level objectives and that even if they *aren't* interested in something—say, the major food crops of Brazil or the principle of subject/verb agreement—they must act as though they are. They learn that their time is not their own and that when the bell rings they must do what is dictated by the "Do Now" or the curriculum-pacing calendar. They learn that everyone must learn the same thing at the same time, that they will be judged on their performance in relation to their peers, and that doing exactly what they are told will ensure their place at or near the top of the pecking order. This is called the "hidden curriculum of schooling" and what it means is that what we think we are teaching and what children are actually learning are quite different things.

Our firstborn had already exhibited a great deal of determination and successful adaptation. By the ripe old age of nine, he had changed his name, demanded a conventional haircut, established himself with peers in four different schools in three different states, and proved himself an able student and a successful competitor in baseball, soccer, and basketball. In hindsight, I needn't have worried about his ability to chart his educational course. But I worried that he might not "keep up" with his age mates, and so in the beginning, I probably helped to create unnecessary tension by wobbling back and forth between freedom and structure. My journal is filled with notes like this:

Monday August 29, 1983
Steve did a few pages in his review workbook on subtraction. Then we went over a page in his subtraction workbook that he had misunderstood and he corrected his work. He read a Hardy Boys mystery for a while. He has not been especially interested in any of my ideas for "book reports" but when I engage him in a discussion on a book he has just finished, he becomes very animated. I try to ask questions about plot, characterization, themes, etc. in the course of the conversation.

Book reports! Shows how conditioned I was to conventional ideas about schooling. Of course, I had all sorts of fabulous ideas about how these could be done. Dioramas. A letter to the author. An advertising poster for the movie version. But none of these things interested him as much as having a good conversation about a book. No surprise. If grown-ups had to do a book report after every novel we read, we'd probably stop reading. Book reports are a feature of institutionalized education, a way for students to prove that they read a book and teachers to figure out if they have comprehended what they read. Of course, there's no better way to assess comprehension than a rich conversation about the reading material, and that is certainly one of the luxuries of learning at home. Fortunately I got over the idea of book reports fairly quickly.

But I couldn't shake some other expectations. Writing, for example. I felt like he should be writing every day. We would do a science experiment and I would suggest that he write about it. He wouldn't be interested. I would suggest writing in a journal. He couldn't figure out what to write. He would ask me for writing assignments. I was tempted to comply. John Holt's spirit whispered in my ear. *It takes time to debrief. Be patient.* Steve did manage to write a fair amount—looking back over my notes, I see places that first year where he fulfilled a number of conventional writing assignments: a paragraph here and there about a trip he took or something he had read, or an exercise from one of the language-arts workbooks that we started out with that first year. But most writing, if it wasn't a letter to his grandparents or a way to keep track of information that he needed, felt contrived—more a way to assuage my concerns than a truly self-initiated activity. And this did not mesh with my budding conviction that writing needed to proceed authentically, from some need to express an idea or work through a thought.

My way of dealing with this tension was to gradually back off. I convinced myself that when he needed to write he would write. And after about a year, I tossed out the grade-level language arts books, with their endless grammar and comprehension exercises that were not connected to any meaningful contexts. I developed a working hypothesis, grounded more in observation and intuition than in any particular theory, that formal academic language could be developed less painfully than through the grueling repetition of linguistic exercises. I figured if we read a lot, and discussed language patterns or rules when they came up in the normal course of events, we could probably cover the basics and he might even retain some of them.

It was slowly dawning on me that if we really want our kids to be engaged, independent, self-reliant, and creative, then we need to trust that they can determine for themselves what is important and how they wish to spend their time. Conventional wisdom dictates that children don't know what is important and cannot make good judgments about how to spend their time, that they need to be persuaded to study and given explicit direction. They need to *learn* to be engaged, independent, self-reliant, creative, etc. But I had raised four toddlers by that time, and it was obvious to me that these creatures were insatiably curious, incredibly persistent, and wildly driven to accomplish challenging new things like climbing up on tables or pouring milk from a gallon jug.

They wanted to know what things tasted like, felt like, sounded like when they hit the floor, how big a splash they could make, basically, how the world works, and they wanted to experience it all to the max! When their speech developed, they were full of questions. *What are you doing? Where does the sky end? Why does the wind blow? How did you get the baby in your tummy?* Just the sort of curiosity one would hope for in an engaged, independent, self-reliant, creative learner. What happens to these self-directed learners when they go to school? All too often, they become apathetic, bored, and disinterested.

"What did you do in school today?"

"Nothing."

"Did you learn anything new?"

"Nope."

There's research that shows that children's excitement about learning peters out by about the third grade. Now that's a sad state of affairs for educators and parents who believe in mission statements, but sadder still for children who have decided that LEARNING IS BORING and that SCHOOL SUCKS.

If learning proceeded seamlessly from toddlerhood, and we merely facilitated, supported, and enriched the natural inclinations of two-year olds as they grew, we might never have to worry about how to get children interested in learning. But the reality is that whether you are a parent deciding to home- or unschool, or a parent of a child in school who has lost interest in learning, questions about motivation and self-direction are pretty high up on your list of concerns. I did not understand it quite so well at the time as I do now, but I was stepping into one of the great modern educational debates about how children learn: In the context of experience? Or as a result of formal systematic training in discrete, sequential skills and isolated bits of knowledge? The formal systematic folks are winning the debate right now, for in a bureaucratic society committed to standardization and regulation, the citizenry must be educated in lockstep. (Okay, we might never achieve the synchronization of fifteen thousand Chinese performers at the Olympics, but that doesn't mean our technocrats and social engineers don't *dream* of such control.) Experience is too unpredictable, outcomes too uncertain to have it any other way. Not to sound like a conspiracy theorist, but if we had a highly personalized approach to learning, people might start thinking their own thoughts. And lord knows where that might lead! All of which is real interesting, considering that Americans regard themselves as extremely individualistic, in comparison, say, to the Chinese. But we're very nervous about really personalizing our education, which has led to a rather peculiar cultural contradiction. While we have, as consumers, endless individual choices about what brand to buy and what to watch on cable television, we also exhibit a surprising conformity of thinking about important aspects of our lives. But I digress.

Where my relaxing of conventional academic requirements led Steve was on a truly personalized and eclectic exploration of a number of topics. Freed of the expectation to document his learning by doing book reports or comprehension exercises, he read voraciously and, to outside eyes, randomly. The seed doesn't fall far from the tree. He averaged a book a day, at times reading up to four on the weekends. Graduating from the Hardy Boys that first year (whew, I breathed a sigh of relief when he exhausted those, even though Yours Truly probably read every Nancy Drew that existed at about the same age), he made his way through Mark Twain, Isaac Asimov, Ray Bradbury, Douglas Adams, and Robert Heinlein. He devoured nonfiction: biographies, and books about space, UFO's, airplanes, computers, the Bermuda Triangle, and baseball. We invested in the *Encyclopedia of Science and Invention*, of which he probably read every volume twice. He was an avid reader of the *Guinness Book of World Records*, and regularly read a number of periodicals cover-to-cover: *Boy's Life, National Geographic World, Science Magazine, Omni, The Mother Earth News, The Farmer's Almanac, the New Age Journal*, and thanks to a subscription my mom got us (what was she thinking?), the *Reader's Digest*, which turned out to be not so bad, in that it allowed us to explore various forms of humor, especially the sentimental, squeaky-clean American brand.

There was no discernible pattern to Steve's reading: it might be baseball history one day, a *Choose Your Own Adventure* book the next, a text about reptiles the next, science fiction the next, and aviation the next. He read in bed and in the car and in the big cedar tree outside our front door (ouch!). I could relate. We had innumerable good conversations about what he was reading. But I did wonder if meaningful learning was going on.

Like most other folks, I was conditioned to think that learning had to be organized in specific ways by experts (we call these the "academic disciplines"), and that the way kids learn actually corresponds to the way these disciplines are structured. This is why the school day is divided into periods—forty-five-minute injections of math and English-language arts and social studies— and it's also why we ascribe an almost religious significance to textbooks. It's no accident that dictionary definitions of the word "discipline" include things like "methods of ensuring that people obey rules by teaching them to do so and punishing them if they do not" or "a controlled orderly state, especially in a class of schoolchildren" or even "punishment designed to teach somebody to obey rules." I'm quite sure that many nine year olds would agree that the textbook study of history constitutes a special brand of punishment.

But don't children *have* to suffer a bit in order to develop their minds? Maybe they don't need to have their knuckles rapped with cane switches or their butts thrashed with paddle boards anymore, like Earl in the Oklahoma schools of the 1950's, or write a hundred times on the blackboard "I will not talk when the teacher is talking" (guess who got to do this!) but learning should definitely not be all fun and games, right? And besides, what are the alternatives?

Thoughtful educators have come up with elegant ideas about how to organize knowledge in ways that might engage the interests of children and help them to make meaningful connections among subjects. These approaches are variously called "theme-based learning," "holistic education," "project-based learning," "problem-based education," or the "core curriculum." No doubt these are improvements over the deadly dullness of the "read the textbook, answer the questions at the end of the chapter, take a quiz" method of instruction. But even these fancy forms of curriculum design mostly disregard the fact that genuine curriculum integration takes place in the mind of the learner, not in the lesson plan, and that we humans have an innate sense of purpose and direction if only life were designed to facilitate our intentions!

I am not opposed to the organization of knowledge into disciplines. In fact, I have taken great pleasure in studying the academic disciplines and appreciate the beauty and elegance of mathematics, history, biology—any number of ways of understanding the world. However, this pleasure was largely derived as an adult, after I had developed the capacity to sit still for long periods of time and revel in abstract ideas. Our mistake is in thinking that such formal ways of learning should be emphasized in the education of young people. I will go so far as to suggest that many of our concerns about education—lack of motivation, classroom-discipline problems, disinterest in learning, failure to retain information—are a direct result of our failure to pay attention to what genuinely interests children and to how they actually think and learn. And I don't mean the kind of learning that is regurgitated on multiple-choice tests and promptly forgotten. I mean the kind of learning that develops independent thinkers, self-reliant workers, and creative problem-solvers. Like in the mission statements.

Thank goodness it did not take Steve four years to be deprogrammed from the hidden curriculum of schooling. Within about a year, he was busy collecting and observing wildlife, raising tadpoles, experimenting with electronics, building models of planes and boats, traveling with his dad on business trips and learning about gemstones, and working out the statistics of his favorite baseball players. And of course, reading ravenously (I *love* words that link reading with hunger). His interests veered towards science, technology, and sports—certainly not my strengths at the time, so I enjoyed those book talks and reveled in learning things alongside of him.

Did he learn to write well? Yes and no. I can't say that he ever developed a particularly strong interest in writing during our unschooling years. There was just too much other interesting stuff to *do!* I can say that when he re-entered school, in the ninth grade, he excelled not just in writing (he was a favorite of his high school English teacher) but in all of his other subjects, none of which, except for math, he had engaged in at all systematically. By the time he was a junior in high school, he had completed advanced placement courses or tested out of most major subject areas, and begun to take courses in physics, calculus, and philosophy at the local state university. By the time he entered college, he had completed almost two years worth of university courses. This was all self-directed activity, which suggests that if we don't bore children to death with formal disciplinary learning in their early years, they just might take to it when the time is right.

There are a couple of other interesting points to make about Steve. First, he has a prodigious memory, which may just be a coincidence or may be connected to his early passion for memorizing facts, stats, or trivia about anything and everything having to do with the longest, tallest, fastest, slowest, shortest, furthest records for climbing, eating, batting, running, accumulating, lifting, parachute jumping, and any number of other human and non-human feats. We are not likely to substitute the *Guinness Book of World Records* for our fourth-grade textbooks any time soon. But in terms of grabbing hold of Steve's interest, there was no contest, and this passion for facts has survived well into his adult years. It's not just a Trivial Pursuit sort of thing either. Steve the grown-up gets passionately interested in certain endeavors—fixed-gear bike racing, craft brewing, gardening, free diving, or arcane-music collecting, to name a few of his leisure pursuits—and he tracks down information and skill relentlessly.

The other thing to note is that Steve has the capacity to put information together in novel, even experimental ways and come up with distinctive theories and explanations for things. Not content with the status quo or the conventional understanding of events or phenomena, he is adept at juxtaposing ideas or putting them together in innovative ways to generate new knowledge, which is the goal of interdisciplinary learning. Whenever I feel "stuck" in conventional thinking about something, I call Steve, who inevitably has a unique or fresh perspective to offer. This is not a capacity that we have figured out how to foster or to assess in our young people, but surely this kind of creative thinking is important to a society such as ours, especially given the enormous challenges—social, environmental, political, economic— we are facing. Could it be that his apparently random selection of topics in those formative years was not random at all, but perhaps guided by some inner sense of what he needed to know to make sense of the world? Did this become a habit of mind, a way of drawing ideas from disparate and, on the surface, disconnected sources to construct new meanings and ways of understanding? It is perhaps telling that one of Steve's intellectual models is Buckminster Fuller, a visionary and futurist who has one of the most original minds of our time and whose thinking is widely interdisciplinary, divergent, and transformative.

I know this sounds a bit like the Lake Woebegone Syndrome, which one critic of homeschooling defined, tongue in cheek, as the idea that "every unschooled child is seen as an above-average self-starter on the verge of genius." In truth, I am not at all sure to what extent Steve's academic and professional successes can be attributed to his unschooling years. After all, it was only a brief (four-year) blip in his school career and he went on to have many skilled and sensitive teachers who knew much more than me in their specialized subject areas.

What I *do* know, is that when he began unschooling, he did not have a strong sense of what he might like to do with his time, nor was he particularly imaginative about how to structure his learning. He had learned well some early lessons from the hidden curriculum of schooling: that others knew what he needed to learn and that he should wait for someone to give him assignments. By the time he re-entered school, four years later, he had become something of an autodidact, with a wide range of interests and pursuits that continued to expand and flourish as he became an adult. In other words, he seriously enjoys learning and is an independent thinker, a self-reliant worker, and a creative problem-solver. What more could a parent hope for, academically speaking? And, by the way, he did learn to write—quite well, in fact—which I attribute to voracious (insatiable…unquenchable…gluttonous) reading. His writing does demonstrate subject/verb agreement. And I suspect he may even know the major food crops of Brazil.

6 The Year of Maps

Of course, a child may not know what he may need to know
in ten years (who does?), but he knows, and much better than
anyone else, what he wants and needs to know right now,
what his mind is ready and hungry for.

~ *John Holt*

WHEN A BABY COMES into this world, they are the very center of the universe, a point of consciousness in a blizzard of shifting colors and smells and shapes and sensations that gradually organize themselves into stable and meaningful objects: breast, eyes, rattle, ball, teddy bear. When the blizzard subsides, the newborn becomes oriented to the more or less stable space she occupies and begins to be intrigued with an ever-expanding universe of objects.

By about the age of six or so, most typically developing children have pretty much figured out their location in space and their relationships to surrounding objects, despite the occasional spilt milk or howling bumps into tabletops. At this point, we assume that they are now developmentally prepared to make the leap to abstraction and identify such objects as "Japan" on a two-dimensional map or a three dimensional globe, and that they can understand such intangible concepts as oceans, equator, continents, and hemispheres. Some children may indeed be successful at the performance indicators that prove they have learned these lessons: identifying latitude and longitude, locating a place on a map, using a map key. But geography is actually a very difficult subject to teach young children, a problem that is further complicated by the fact that little time is devoted to it in most schools, which are currently more concerned with upping the test scores in literacy and mathematics.

It would not have occurred to me that the study of geography might become a major focus of our first year of unschooling, but observing carefully how this interest emerged and evolved was a key factor in my understanding that often one of the most effective forms of instruction might best be described as "getting out of the way." My initial contribution was to post two large maps, one of the US and one of the world, on our unfinished sheetrock walls. Given that we didn't really have television reception in Paradise, the boys spent a lot of time gazing at these. Steve, with his prodigious memory, had already mastered the board game "Name That State" and beat me so regularly that I felt compelled to document it the first time that I beat him. But this was about the extent of my commitment to geography as subject matter.

One day in August of our first year, Shaman decided he wanted to draw a map of Oklahoma. But he changed his mind and decided to draw one of the property we lived on, which in hindsight was a striking example of the need to start with the familiar before branching out. So all of the boys and I went for a long walk to explore the lay of the land. Oklahoma may be one of the easiest places on the planet to do this, thanks to the pragmatic planning of the bureaucrats who decreed that all lands ceded by American Indians to the government of the United States were to be subdivided into sections (640 acres or one square mile) laid out on a grid like a checkerboard. Quarter sections of 160 acres were the size of most of the nineteenth-century homesteads that white settlers staked out for themselves in the big land grabs. Six square miles equals thirty-six sections equals a township. A miracle of modern rational planning. By the time we settled our little corner of Paradise Township, the state of Oklahoma, in addition to being thoroughly overgrazed, overmined, overdrilled, and pumped out, had also been systematically sectioned off and divided up. Our piece of land, a mere twenty acres, was accessed by a dirt driveway off the main dirt section road (which by the way, all turned to sticky, sloshing red mud during hard rains).

That August day, we walked down the drive, which was bounded on either side with large eastern red cedar trees, a beautiful pest species that hogs more than its share of water and wreaks havoc on native plant communities. When we got to the section road, we stood in the middle of it, which was not dangerous because few living souls ever drove out that way, and if they did, you could hear them a mile off. We talked about the cardinal directions—north, south, east, and west—and ritually turned to face each of them. And partly because I want to help balance out the karmic crime of stealing and dividing up native lands into six-mile-square tracts, and partly because I want our boys to develop a profound appreciation for the many ways that people have devised to remind themselves that life is sacred, I tell them that the Cherokee, from whom they are descended through their father, believed that there were actually seven cardinal directions, including in addition to the usual four, above, below, and the center (us). We talk a bit about the fact that the Cherokee assigned colors to the directions (east/red, west/black, south/white, north/blue) and pondered why they might have made those choices. I mention that the directions, to many native people, were part of a religious way of understanding the world and their place in it. We talk about more practical things too, like where the sun rises and where it sets, which direction certain towns were in, and so forth. On our walk back, I remind Steve how we used to make haiku poetry on our walks in the New Mexico forest four years ago, and he astonishes me by reciting one of these. We make plans to do some haiku the next day. And that was about it, in terms of geography study, for the next month or so.

In October, Steve, Shaman, and I read a couple of library books about the geography of Oklahoma and made a plan to create relief maps. Making relief maps is actually one of my most lucid and pleasurable memories from elementary school, which is an indication to me that something important (like being permitted to get your fingers all mucky) might be involved. So in this instance I initiated an activity that the boys got reasonably excited about, and we made a list of necessary supplies. One day in mid-October, we finished the maps, nicely embellished with painted rivers, lakes, and flags denoting their favorite places.

Later that day, Shaman took most of the afternoon to draw a painstakingly accurate map of Oklahoma, with all seventy-seven counties, each colored in a different color. I was stunned, mostly because it hadn't occurred to me that a child would be interested in learning the *counties* of a state. A county, after all, is a real low-life—not a city, not a state, but some kind of in-between creature, with functions that are mostly mysterious to everyone except the election board and the road crews. But Shaman was fascinated with counties and drew these maps repeatedly. Capitalizing on the interest in counties, I bought a large Oklahoma county map to add to our collection on the sheetrock walls. One day in October, we were in the midst of statewide flooding from a Mexican hurricane. Whenever we heard on the radio about an affected county, we stuck in a pushpin, and soon our living room took on the appearance of a political organizing headquarters. Our county map and pushpins also served us well in tornado season—as I've said, we lived smack dab in the middle of Tornado Alley—and we eagerly tracked radio reports of blockbuster winds headed in our direction. This was truly learning with an essential purpose, of which there is far too little in schools.

Both Shaman and Steve stayed interested in geography, poring over maps when we traveled, either as a family or with their dad when he took them along on trips to sell gemstones. We became scavengers of maps, visiting the Chamber of Commerce to collect regional maps, raiding our collection of *National Geographic* for the maps, and sending off to every agency we could find that provided free ones, until we had a very large box full. Steve's approach to learning geography was to have me create tests, which I enjoyed making and he enjoyed taking. I would even sneak in some essay questions to make sure he had to do some writing. Tests? Unschoolers? Well sure, I'm happy to give a kid a test *at their invitation.* There is nothing inherently wrong with tests and they are quite good at determining whether we can remember things on demand, especially isolated bits of information. They are not so good at determining whether we have made meaning out of something or whether we can really apply what we know.

Shaman was not particularly interested in taking tests. He *was* interested in drawing maps, so interested in fact that it constituted the major component of his curriculum for the next year. He soon graduated from Oklahoma counties to freehand-drawn maps of the United States. He would sometimes spend the entire day and on into the night, making multiple copies, starting over whenever he wasn't completely satisfied. He drew over two hundred maps that year. On Thanksgiving, he drew the first of many accurate, freehand maps of the United States *from memory.* No props. I swear it. Not even in the same room as the wall map. And he repeated this activity over and over and over again. I could see little variation in the maps, but evidently he could, or else he just wanted to perfect his skill. Seldom did a day go by without its share of new maps. We ran out of space to display them on the sheetrock.

One activity that thoroughly engaged him almost daily for a year was looking up a state in the encyclopedia and reading everything there was to read about it. The choices seemed fairly arbitrary—it might be Kansas one day and New York the next, states along the Mississippi River one day and Springfield, Ohio the next. Springfield, Ohio? Go figure. Then he would draw various maps of that state or region or city; perhaps one with rivers or one with lakes, one with the mountain ranges or one with the major cities. He made books about such exciting topics as "Illinois." His reading choices at the library were almost entirely nonfiction books with such thrilling titles as—you guessed it—"Texas," "Arkansas," and "Florida." He particularly enjoyed one-upping me by marking but not naming cities on the state maps he drew and then testing me to see if I could guess correctly, which I occasionally did.

In December, he shifted from the states and regions of the US to other continents, working into the wee hours of the night drawing maps of Africa, Australia, South America, North America, Asia, and Europe. Asking thousands of questions (*What kind of government does Nicaragua have? How long is the Amazon River? Which way does it run? How are mountains made? Is China our ally? Why do the borders change on different maps?*) Children's capacity to *question* astounds me and I can't figure out why we don't construct the entire school curriculum around their wonderful questions (I have, in fact, in my many years of working with teachers, met an amazing few who do just this, with extraordinary results). Shaman went through reams of paper, drawing maps of every conceivable spot on this planet. My desire to preserve trees battled my fascination with this journey he was on. Here's a journal description of a typical day:

Tuesday December 6
Shaman got started on map drawing with fervor this morning. Indeed, it was difficult to drag him to the breakfast table for a pancake breakfast! He did four maps this morning—one of the United States, one of the US, Alaska and Canada (with provinces), one of Australia, and one of the world (a sphere). This last one was particularly interesting to me because he drew the globe from the perspective of the sun at 3:00 a.m. (our time.) This launched a discussion about which way the Earth spins, why we have time zones, what causes the seasons, etc.

I'm not sure why my entry sounds so blasé —I mean, I *was* trying to be objective, merely recording events without a lot of interpretation in case the authorities ever wanted to know what we were up to. But I should have been jumping up and down! In just three months, a "first-grade child" had gone from learning the cardinal directions while standing in the middle of our section road to representing the planet in its geographical entirety (from memory), and further, had figured out the spatial and temporal relationships between Spaceship Earth and its solar Mother Ship. And indeed, his interests expanded to astronomy and the solar system from this point on. But that's not the whole of the earthly geography story.

Early on, in October, Shaman had begun studying our large atlas in earnest, initiating conversations about big concepts such as area, perimeter, population, and boundaries. He took special pleasure in comparing states and countries by size and population, and found it necessary to learn alphabetical order (a discovery he made on his own) while doing this. I would find him late at night, poring over the atlas in the top bunk of the bed he shared with Räm. *What could he possibly be doing?* I wondered. Turns out what he was doing was making a self-initiated quantum leap in his mathematical abilities.

His math curriculum to that point had mostly involved playing around with math manipulatives—creating colorful equations with Cuisenaire Rods, designing geometric art with pattern blocks, and working out the four arithmetic operations with chips or cubes. I was taking it slow, hoping to generate a love of mathematics through a more experiential approach than my own rote learning of the subject, which unfortunately had led to a deep antipathy towards math. We casually worked on cardinal and ordinal numbers, more-than and less-than, odds and evens, place value, measurement, and simple fractions, most often with games or objects and whenever possible within the context of some meaningful experience like measuring the garden to build raised beds for vegetables or baking a cake, which was at the top of his list of favorite things to do. He occasionally did some paper and pencil work with numbers in a workbook.

Despite my relaxed pace, within the course of that year—now listen carefully— he taught himself to calculate sums and compare values using all four of the basic mathematical operations... into the millions…through studying the atlas. I AM NOT KIDDING! He relished working out comparative math problems that he generated from looking at lists of populations, areas in square miles, and other demographic details. Here's an example:

Wednesday May 2
This morning Shaman started out reading the selection on Rhode Island in the World Book. *He got out his solar calculator and was working with it for a long time while looking at the encyclopedia. He was adding up the populations of all the counties, and then subtracting that figure from the total population to find out if the resulting figure corresponded to the total population of the unincorporated areas.*

Now this is not a math problem that you would generally find in a first-grade math workbook. The fact that he generated the problem himself is a powerful argument for interdisciplinary curriculum (in this case, exploring mathematics and geography alongside each other) but even more than that, it convinced me that when children need to know some particular skill in order to understand something they care about, they will grab hold of it. In this case, his efforts to compare geographical entities, whether in terms of their size or their population, simply could not be accomplished without some further skill development with numbers. So, with very little input from me, he quickly mastered a number of relevant mathematical concepts.

Keep in mind that this was a kid who was still, at the time that he was developing multistep math problems to solve, working to master the art of cursive handwriting. Children's development is profoundly uneven—they can be precociously advanced in one area and on quite the same level as peers in others, which is a strong argument *against* trying to teach a group of age peers all the same things at the same pace at the same time. It's also worth mentioning that an almost daily activity during this time, for which he recruited eager younger brothers Räm and Chris, was building cities with a variety of materials—small wooden blocks and large red cardboard bricks, dominoes, pattern blocks, Lincoln Logs, toilet paper rolls—whatever was at hand, mixed and matched. Sometimes much of the day was spent in such constructions. Now few classrooms beyond the preschool level have such materials available, or if they do, they are seldom used. Building with blocks is seen as frivolous, nonessential. However, as Shaman was busy with more sophisticated studies of mathematics and geography, he still felt a strong need to play with building materials to reinforce his learning. And he and everyone else lived for the days when I would let them build volcanoes, fill them with baking soda and vinegar and red food coloring, and watch them explode, preferably with lava tumbling down onto a recently built city!

I think we are making a humongous mistake eliminating play in favor of the presumably more rigorous academic curriculum for our younger elementary students. In many kindergarten and first-grade classrooms in New York City, where I now live and teach, there is no longer time or materials for dramatic play, block building, recess, clay pounding, tempera painting, or singing. Instead, children sit scrunched over their papers, writing and erasing and revising their "small moments" and practicing filling in the bubbles on multiple-choice worksheets. We've got to get them ready for the real world of reading, writing, and tests. Not only is this borderline abusive, it is inefficient! Play is essential to a number of cognitive functions in the development of young children. Play creates mental images, which are vital components of concept formation (*How are cities laid out? What is an electricity grid?*). Play allows youngsters to manipulate variables (*What happens when a bridge is not adequately supported? What if the water supply runs out?*) or experiment with possibilities (*How should streets be laid out for the most efficient travel? Where should there be traffic signals?*). All of these questions were posed and explored as my boys built their cities.

In the Year of Maps, play and free exploration resulted in the informal acquisition of innumerable advanced concepts: area, perimeter, population, boundaries, borders, equator, continents, hemispheres, latitude, longitude, etc. and in a number of advanced mathematical skills. None of these things were *taught* per se, they were *acquired* because they were felt by the learner to be necessary to his further understanding of something he was obviously interested in. And all of this happened through the study of a topic for which we allocate very little actual time in the usual classroom, which indicates to me that the "basics" might very well be mastered in more roundabout ways than we believe.

Footnote #1: Meaningful learning experiences can sometimes translate into generative action. Note this excerpt from my journal at the end of The Year of Maps:

Thursday May 3
Shaman read about Montana and Minnesota in the encyclopedia this morning. He then made a model with blocks of one of the main streets in our town (University Ave.) complete with traffic and parked cars (hot wheels). It was a spatially accurate representation. He then spent the rest of the morning laboring over a letter to our representative in Congress. Here's the text of it:

Dear Wes,
I hope you can do something about cities growing too big. What I'm mainly concerned about is that all our good lakes will get polluted. And all our good farms will be surrounded by cities. If too many cities grow too big, there won't be enough water for everyone.
Only the rich and middle class will be able to afford good water. And if some of the cities close to the Canadian border get too polluted the Canadians will get mad. If only the US will start spending more money on getting water instead of spending so much money on military equipment.
Yours truly,
Shaman Hatley

Footnote #2: People tend to retain things that they learn *if they study things that they are interested in*. Shaman entered public school in what would have been his sixth-grade year, but which turned out to be a complicated combination of seventh- and eighth-grade classes because his almost entirely self-directed learning experiences had resulted in the easy mastery of much of the junior high curriculum. Between the end of The Year of Maps and that time he paid relatively little attention to geography, having moved on to other passions. But in school that year, he managed to recall enough information to win a schoolwide geography contest without studying even a tiny bit.

Most of the teachers I know agonize because children do not remember things from year to year, or week to week, or even day to day. (Some might say minute to minute!) It is just possible that children do not remember things because *they do not care about them*. Some students have the discipline or the training or the parental pressure to force themselves to care so that they can regurgitate the information on a test, but I will be so bold as to say that children do not care about a huge proportion of what they are expected to remember in school. Shaman remembered his basic geography, and he remembered it pretty well. For whatever reason, geography was the organizing center of his first-grade year and five years later, it was still fresh in his mind. I suspect this is because *he cared* about it. I don't know *why* he cared about it so much and for so long. All I can say is that there was some sort of internal compass at work, guiding him along a conceptual journey that began on a sunny summer day on our section road and took him in ever-widening spheres from our land to the town, to the county, to the state, to the country, to the world, and on out to the solar system. This, in fancy educational language, was the scope and sequence of his first-grade curriculum, and it was definitely not ordained in any curriculum guidebook save that of his little six-year-old soul.

7 The Long-Term View

Study without desire spoils the memory, and it retains nothing that it takes in.

~ Leonardo da Vinci

IT'S A CLICHÉ, BUT education really *is* a lifelong journey. While formal schooling has endpoints for most people, we continue to learn until we die. We engage with objects and people and animals and nature and images and text in our environment, and our cognition changes as a result. Hopefully, we also act on these new ideas, and then the environment changes as a result and other people learn from *our* created objects and words and images and texts. That's why learning is said to be a social thing. Dewey called these activities *transactions*, and while schooling aims to do this in a systematic way, informal learning is always going on both in and out of school.

Too often, we label children as failures when they don't perform on demand according to an arbitrary schedule determined by experts. But young people have their own unique timetables as well as highly individualized intelligence profiles. Schools pay lip service to the idea that children have different learning styles. And many teachers work very hard to "differentiate instruction," which means figuring out varied ways to communicate information and otherwise facilitate learning. But the reality is that we hold very narrow visions of what counts as learning and stigmatize children who do not conform to these expectations. Our stigmatization can be benevolent—we label it "assessment of student needs" or "remediation" but the message is the same: *you are not ok the way you are, and we need to fix you.*

Räm was in a rush from the day he was born. We had moved back to Oklahoma from our New Mexico mountain retreat, in part so that Earl could develop a sales territory in Oklahoma, and in part to be closer to a birthing center. After a hair-raising home birth with Shaman two years before that ended up in a hospital emergency room (he chose to enter—or in his case not enter—the world in full lotus posture, butt first), we were trying to be better prepared for difficulties this time. We packed up our worldly belongings late in the pregnancy, drove a U-haul trailer through a treacherous mountain blizzard, rented a house in Stillwater, and found a birth center with midwives and an attending physician who was a dedicated advocate of natural and home birth. The birth center was a mere forty-five-minute drive down I-40 to Oklahoma City from our house, which seemed like ample time.

Two years before, I'd been in labor for six hours with Shaman, so I assumed this one would be similar. Thinking I had all the time in the world with Räm, I piddled around after that first gentle contraction, waiting fifteen minutes for the bread to come out of the oven. I called my friend Melissa, who planned to come with us to help with childcare at the birthing center, and then we loaded up the car with Steve, Shaman, and the new baby gear and picked her up at her house. Halfway to Oklahoma City, I realized that I was in what labor specialists call transition (contractions coming hot and heavy while baby makes his way down the birth canal). It didn't seem possible that this baby was going to arrive only thirty minutes after the first contraction, but like I said, the kid was in a hurry from the start. My memory is a bit cloudy on the fine points here, so I can't remember who first came up with the idea that we needed to pull off the highway and deliver the baby. I do remember Earl having a heck of a time pulling over, seeing that we were driving in the fast lane during rush hour, which would prove to be an excellent metaphor for Räm's personality.

We finally managed to pull over—it was probably only a few minutes, but they seemed like *long* minutes— and landed in the parking lot of a big truck stop. Melissa hopped out and Earl walked around to the passenger side. And there on the green vinyl front seat of our Ford F150 Supercab, in the parking lot of an Oklahoma truck stop, with six-year-old Steve and two-and-a-half-year-old Shaman peering over the back seat, Räm made his hasty appearance. He was a bit blue, having made such a precipitous descent that he'd managed to get himself tangled up in the umbilical cord. Earl, with those nerves of steel and steady hands, had reached in and unwrapped it from around his neck. My main memory from this moment was hearing my linguistically precocious toddler ask, in a slightly disdainful tone of voice, "Mom, don't you think there's a better place to do this?"

We refused the offer of an ambulance from the state trooper who had seen something curious and pulled up. Considering that we didn't have any way to tie off and cut the cord, we hightailed it to the birthing center with the trooper clearing the way for us, me holding Ram up high to facilitate the blood flow in the proper direction and pink him up a bit. Earl found a pay phone when we got there and called up to the office. The unflappable midwives came down and delivered the placenta in the parking lot. We then took the elevator up to their clinic where I showered and we got checked out, and then headed home to dinner with fresh baked, still warm whole wheat bread. Like I said, Räm was in a hurry. His birth certificate, in the "Location of Birth" space, reads Hwy. I-40.

Other than the inevitable variations that have to do with birth order, Räm's early childhood upbringing was pretty much like that of his older brothers. However, his temperament was not exactly what you would call cuddly, which I had come to expect as normal. When they were infants, Steve and Shaman took full advantage of nursing time to relax, savor every drop, take little gurgle-and-smile breaks, and beam up at me with devoted eyes. Even when they weren't hungry, they wanted to glom on to their human pacifier. Räm, on the other hand, would gulp and guzzle just as fast as he possibly could, then launch himself away from me, projectile vomit and look around for something else to do. He started crawling at about six months, got bored with that, and just past the eight month milestone, stood up for about a day and then walked across the room. One afternoon, after he had just turned one, I looked out in the yard to see Steve and Shaman teaching him to dribble the soccer ball.

Howard Gardner (the developmental psychologist who came up with the theory of multiple intelligences) would say Räm had a strong kinesthetic intelligence. Not only was he physically skilled, he was fearless. While Shaman stood alongside the playground slide for about a year and a half, calculating the relationship between slope and speed in his toddler brain, Räm scrambled up the ladder the minute he could and whizzed down like a bullet. He took to Steve's Big Wheel like he was born to the racetrack. When Shaman joined the local kindergarten soccer team, the coach caught a glimpse of Räm dribbling on the sidelines, and surreptitiously recruited my not-yet-four year old for the team, where he proceeded to run like a rabbit being chased by hound dogs down the field and rack up the goals.

Räm was not opposed to listening to stories. However, when we read he did not snuggle up and rest his head on my shoulder like the other boys did. He always had to have something in his hands to fiddle with, usually a Hot Wheels car or a Star Wars action figure. I was mildly annoyed at this, wondering why I wasn't getting his undivided attention with my clever character voices and meaningful intonations. Then one day, when I asked him something about the story and discovered that he had almost perfect recall of it, I realized that he *was* totally attentive, and that twiddling objects was merely his way of focusing. Though he enjoyed stories and word play, he was unresponsive to the tactics I had used with his older brothers to introduce them to the fundamentals of reading, such as stopping and pointing to a word to sound out while reading. Whenever I attempted to "teach" him how to read, he would smile broadly at me, his eyes gleaming with the excitement that seemed to permanently inhabit his body. His legs would start pumping up and down and the twiddling would start in earnest. His body language was telling me in no uncertain terms, "This is not what I want to be doing." We called him Räm the Bomb. Still do.

Fortunately, I had come to terms with the reality that kids were not always eager to do the things you thought they should be doing, so I was able to let go of my expectations and just engage in the ways he wanted to engage. But when he was about seven, I was itching with the thought that he just might not ever want to learn to read. He still liked listening to books, though he continued fiddling with objects. He liked to draw and would sometimes write a word or two, or even a sentence on his drawings. But when I made a move that could conceivably be interpreted as reading instruction, to work with him on digraphs or diphthongs, he'd be off the couch with a leap to catch the cat, or play with those darned Star Wars action figures. As we approached the end of what would have been first grade, I was getting discouraged. Clearly something was not clicking with him in the reading department.

Steve had built up quite a collection of Hardy Boys books over the years, teenage adventure stories geared towards the middle-school reader. One day, when he was approaching eight, Räm came into the living room with a Hardy Boys mystery in his hands, plopped down beside me on the couch, and said, "I'm gonna read this to you." Humoring him, I said, "Okay!" and he opened the book to the first chapter. Without an error, he read the first page. All right, I thought, Steve read it to him and he must have memorized it. Then he read the next page and the next. Dumfounded, I listened. He had intonation. Read with fluency. I called everyone over. We all listened. We marveled. We cheered. And I humbly reassessed my worries about his reading timetable. Räm had clearly skipped over some of the conventional steps, like systematic phonics instruction, though I had occasionally managed to note the presence of a compound word before he scurried away. And despite what looked on the surface like some sort of attention deficit disorder—though I would have eaten dirt before I would have uttered those words— he had clearly been absorbing lots of information about the process of reading. I considered this a minor miracle, and from that time on, he was engaged with the usual chapter books that kids a year or two older than he were reading. As an eight-year-old nonreader, he would have been a candidate for Reading Recovery in school and suffered all the humiliation and loss of self-esteem that occurs when kids feel like they are not "making the grade." As it was, he entered the third grade as a fluent reader and proceeded to do just fine in elementary school.

I truly do believe that children have a natural affinity for learning. It's what they're programmed to do. If they're resistant to learning, it's probably because they've been forced or coerced or are otherwise just *not ready* to learn a particular thing at a particular time. Reading, like anything else, comes at different times for different people, and this is now confirmed by recent research on the brain. Apparently there is not a magic window that exists in which we have to learn how to read or lose the opportunity. Lots of kids, both schooled and unschooled, are not ready to read at age five or six, even if they've been prepped by phonics flash cards in the crib. In school, such children are labeled "slower" learners, or worse yet, learning disabled, and made to endure extra practice, special classes, more homework, and tutoring because they *must catch up*. It damages their self-esteem, squashes that natural love of learning, and turns something that should be fun into a painful and difficult chore. And for what? Maybe that child would have learned to read easily, naturally, if he were allowed to do so in another six months, or a year. Or two. And let's say one child begins reading at age four, and another begins reading at age nine. When they're both thirty, would you be able to tell which was which? Probably not.

Räm coped well with the public school system when he did start school, though the academic work never truly turned him on. Often bored, he lived for the last bell when he could come home, put on his rollerblades or grab his skateboard and tear down the steep hills of Montpelier, Vermont, where we moved when he was thirteen. Every Friday in winter, his school transported the kids to Sugar Bush Mountain for skiing. There was never any trouble getting him out of bed on a Friday morning. On other winter days, Räm was home and in his snow gear immediately after school, and he and his friends snowboarded for hours down every hill in the community. He and Chris both stayed out long after the early Vermont dark set in, and came home soggy, red-cheeked, and happy. Homework was an afterthought.

A star soccer player all through school, Räm was the kid that annually earned the "Forward of the Year" award. Just like when he was on Shaman's kindergarten team, the path always seemed to clear magically before him, and he would streak down the field and shoot the ball squarely into the net. He was unstoppable. Until he hit high school algebra. He tried twice to pass that course. It just had him stymied. Perhaps an extra hour of homework every night would have gotten him through. But there were so many other more captivating things to do. When he *did* come in the house, ruddy and hungry from snowboarding or rollerblading or bicycling, there were all those musical instruments waiting for him upstairs. He and Chris had the whole top floor of our Victorian for their motley collection of drums, electric guitars, amplifiers, keyboards, violins, saxophones, clarinets, and whatever other instrument they could get their hands on. Turned out that Räm had a finely tuned ear. And an uncanny instinct for picking up just about any musical instrument and getting some good sounds out of it. In high school, he was the drummer for both the concert band and the jazz ensemble. Between soccer, band, and Friday skiing, he had good reasons to get up and go to school every morning. As with many young people, the co-curricular activities meant the difference between engagement with school and disengagement.

In his junior year, after celebrating his annual "Forward of the Year" recognition, Räm was informed that he would no longer be eligible for soccer because of that algebra grade. I protested, anticipating the effect this decision would have on him. No use—rules were rules, and he would just have to suffer the consequences. Never mind that he had such well-developed musical, artistic, kinesthetic, and interpersonal intelligences. These are simply not valued as much as mathematics. Predictably, this misfortune initiated a downhill spiral, which culminated in him dropping out of high school a year before graduating. He lost that spark, that zest for living every moment to its fullest that I loved about him. With my encouragement, he enrolled in a local pottery class. He made macramé jewelry and snowboarded once winter came. But he was adrift.

We had moved to Vermont when I was offered a position on the faculty of Goddard College, a small, progressive liberal arts school. I had turned down other offers, in part for the quality of life this beautiful state offered, and in part because of my past association with Goddard during those heady days of Flaming Rainbow. Goddard was significantly subdued since the wild experimentalism of the sixties and seventies, and had become quite a bit more structured, but had stayed true to its fundamental principles: students should have a great deal of say over what and how they learn, evaluation is a negotiated process between faculty and students, and learning should be grounded in real life experiences. Räm completed his GED, applied to Goddard, and was accepted. It was absolutely the best thing that could have happened to him. He played in the jazz band, studied medieval history and green woodworking with a Smithsonian scholar, and finally had a writing teacher who celebrated what he had to say and knew just the right formula for constructive criticism. He recovered his zest for living and learning in this environment that nourished the individual and their unique intelligences. He did not complete his undergraduate work at Goddard, but was awarded a BA in Jazz Performance from Long Island University, where he was fortunate to study with some of the best contemporary jazz artists in New York City.

Here's the clincher. Other than having to successfully complete the basic math component of the GED, Räm successfully avoided math since the algebra debacle that had ended both his glorious soccer run and his high school career. When faced with having to complete the only remaining requirements for his BA, the dreaded math credits, he stayed out of school for a semester and worked the restaurant job that supported him through college. Finally, caving to maternal persuasion, he took the math placement test and scored rather high. He enrolled in the required math course, and at the end of the semester was somewhat stunned to receive an A along with a note from the professor stating that he seemed to have a real aptitude for mathematics. Go figure. If that high school algebra teacher had done a better job of reaching him, or if kinesthetic skills were valued as much as calculative abilities, Räm the Bomb might have made the National Men's Soccer team. Or not. As it turned out, Räm harbored another undiscovered perceptual skill in addition to his finely tuned ear—a finely tuned palate and a keen memory for the subtleties of hundreds of varieties of wine. After taking post-graduate classes in viticulture and enology and working his way up in the industry, he is now, in addition to being a successful musician, a well-established wine consultant in the Napa Valley.

What would it mean to truly take a long-term view of young people's learning? Taking a long-term view would mean that we honor the unique timetables that govern people's developing abilities. Children are not seals. We should not label them as failures when they do not perform on demand. They are also not automobile engines that must be *serviced* when they are broken. Much of our educational thinking is based on children's perceived deficits rather than their perceived strengths. Taking the long-term view would mean that we focus more on what children *can* do than what they *can't* do. This in itself would revolutionize educational practice. It does *not* mean that we should imbue children with a false sense of self-esteem through undeserved praise, or give them an exalted sense of their abilities. It means working with their strengths to build other capacities. Kids develop a strong sense of self when they have a sense of personal agency and autonomy, when they accomplish their goals, when they are respected, and when they receive accurate feedback on their work. Taking a long-term view would mean that we value the full range of intelligences equally, even if we risk having a society composed solely of jazz musicians or wine tasters or soccer players. (Won't happen, but wouldn't that be fun?) It would mean that we work diligently with all kids to help them discover and cultivate those interests and talents that will give them the courage and stamina to stick with tasks that are hard or do not offer immediate gratification. We now know that people will change jobs/careers/professions multiple times in an average lifetime and that rapid social and technological change will be the norm. We know we must be a *lifelong-learning society* if we are to meet these challenges. So, if we know that learning is going to be a lifelong process, and that human development itself is a lifelong process, we need to think seriously about what those twelve years of childhood that we have earmarked for "school" should look like. Should they be a curricular assembly line, turning out predictable, quality-controlled products? Or should they be a special period in life where people discover their passions and purposes and interests and capacities, so that they might develop into passionate, purposeful, interesting, and skilled human beings? We must remember to not mindlessly equate success in school with success in life. After all, some moderately brilliant and productive people did poorly or dropped out of school. Thomas Edison. Benjamin Franklin. Walt Disney. Colonel Sanders. Elton John. And Houdini.

8 Animal Farm

"...there is a profound, inescapable need for animals that is in all people everywhere, an urgent requirement for which no substitute exists."

~ *Paul Shepard*

THE COLFAX FAMILY OF homeschooling fame homesteaded forty-seven acres of California wilderness and successfully steered three of their four sons to Ivy League institutions where they obtained advanced degrees and went on to illustrious careers in medicine and law. David and Micki Colfax's book, *Homeschooling for Excellence*, came out after our unschooling experience, so we did not benefit from their wisdom, but Grant, John, Reed, and Garth Colfax became poster children for a generation of home and unschoolers. Much of their academic distinction derived from their extensive and successful experiences with animal husbandry. Like the Colfaxes, we aimed for self-sufficiency, albeit on a smaller parcel of land, and always assumed that the care and breeding of animals would be an essential part of the plan. We did give it our best shot, and we certainly learned a lot from our efforts, but unlike the Colfaxes, it would be a stretch to claim any distinction whatsoever in the realm of raising animals, with the possible exception of tadpoles.

Before I met Earl, my experience of caring for domestic creatures had been limited to guppies that died within days of their purchase, an Easter chick who did not survive the summer in my suburban backyard wading pool, and the family dachshund, Gufuffnick Garfinkle, who, when his back legs got paralyzed, had to be walked in a sling. I did have a brief and disastrous relationship once with a guy who decided we should buy ourselves horses to ride through the Sebastopol apple orchards around his remote northern California cabin. Clancy (that's the horse) and I got along fine and I learned how to pick the rocks out of his hoofs and brush him down after riding, but the fellow and I did not get along as well, so my equestrian experience was short-lived.

My family often went on trout fishing vacations in the Rocky Mountains, so I was not naïve about what was involved in catching, killing, and consuming animals. Earl, raised in rural Oklahoma and Arkansas, grew up with a gun in one hand and a fishing pole in the other, and most of the folks he knew raised chickens and pigs and cows. But like many others in the sixties counterculture, we had rejected meat eating on moral, philosophical, and health grounds. When we met, I was ripe for conversion from my fruitarianism to Earl's more sensible lacto-vegetarian diet, so while we weren't interested in killing our nonhuman brothers and sisters, we were happy to consume their reproductive by-products (i.e. milk).

When I was pregnant with Steve, we lived for a short time on a rural yoga ashram/farm near Skiatook, Oklahoma. As hippie communes went, things worked well, probably because no one was taking drugs or sleeping with other people's partners. It also helped that a number of the residents had grown up on Midwestern farms. We enjoyed a surfeit of fresh butter and creamy yogurt thanks to a herd of friendly goats, and I thoroughly enjoyed playing milkmaid. What every vegetarian goat farmer must eventually come to grips with, however, is what to do with the male offspring of these gentle and affectionate nannies. The yogis had been paralyzed by the moral contradictions presented by the resident billy goat. Clearly, it would be wrong to kill the smelly creature (and male goats do stink, terribly, and the stink flavors the milk of their mothers and sisters if they wander within shouting distance). They could keep it for breeding, but with such a small operation, it wouldn't be worth a fraction of the cost of his feed. They could castrate it, but then it would serve no discernible purpose but to escape the fence and eat everything in sight, including the struggling new fruit trees. By the time we arrived in the community, the adorable little guy had been allowed to live off the fruits of the land until he had become a huge, stinking, belligerent, over-sexed buck.

Earl and the Goats, Skiatook, Oklahoma, circa 1972

One night, Earl and I were returning to our primitive cabin from evening meditation in the main ashram building. My belly was the size of a prize-winning Oklahoma watermelon, and I made my way down the dirt path by waddling from side to side. Earl had a large flashlight to illuminate the opossums, raccoons, bats, and other nocturnal creatures we were likely to encounter. Suddenly we heard galloping hooves on the path behind us. What could it be? Earl spun around and shined the flashlight beam but it was too late; that buck had reared itself up and knocked me flat on my watermelon belly. Thank goodness for the flashlight— Earl went into warrior mode and beat that creature around the ears until he ran off to do whatever other damage he could find to do. I was shaken, to say the least, and it was a stroke of good luck that I did not go into early labor. To this day, I am the only person I know that has been assaulted by a goat.

You would think the attack of the billy goat would have deterred us from goat farming, but two years later, when were living in that army tent, we decided to give it another try. Conditions were primitive but things were progressing. We had a productive garden and had built a chicken house and a goat shed, if not a people house. We were given a very sweet, pregnant doe and in due time she gave birth. To a male. This time, there would be no moral wavering. Uncle River had come to stay with us, and he and Earl determined that meat eating would be acceptable if one was prepared to take responsibility for the whole nine yards— the killing, the butchering, and the use of every possible particle of the animal, including the eventual tanning of its hide.

While I was off doing something or other, hoeing the garden or washing clothes in a circa 1940 wringer washer that I filled with cold water from the hose, Earl and Uncle River did the deed. I didn't even know about it until some time later, when Steve, who had been playing in the woods, came into the tent with a horrified expression on his face and tears streaming down his cheeks. He had come across poor Billy hanging from a tree, dripping blood. I know kids the world over participate in the killing of animals, and it's just a natural part of life, but my little vegetarian kid was traumatized. Totally inadequate parenting, not to have prepared him for this. I too was distressed by the sight of the creature, who only a day ago had been cavorting about the underbrush and sticking his nose through the garden fence to munch the baby spinach and wild lambs-quarters. I dutifully helped to cook the stew, and tried one small stringy bite, but lost my stomach for goat farming.

Years later, when we tried homesteading for the second time in Paradise, we were slightly more grounded in the realities of a life of self-sufficiency, opting to first construct a shelter for our large family before taking on the additional burden of animals. We imagined someday having a flock of chickens for fresh eggs, but for now, the garden was enough of a responsibility. However, the boys were pestering us to eat meat. I was open to it, thinking that moderation was probably a sound operating principle. I had observed too many vegetarian friends' children sneaking hot dogs at picnics and figured we might as well let the kids work out for themselves what they would eat. But we did want them to be aware of what is involved. So, twenty-seven years before Mark Zuckerberg declared his intention to only eat meat that he himself had killed, we decided on the same strategy. When Earl was not on the road selling gemstones, he began taking his sons fishing in local lakes and ponds and streams.

The boys exhibited no moral qualms about this, and their anatomy studies really took off as they cleaned and prepared the catfish, bass, and bluegill that began to supplement our fresh vegetable and whole-grain diet. Not content merely to go fishing, Steve devoured every available library book on the topic, including the entire *Encyclopedia of Fishing* two times through. He studied the conditions that were conducive to catching fish, analyzing water temperature, flow, and depth. He observed and kept track of weather patterns, barometric pressure, and water clarity. He documented what kind of bait different fish liked, where they hid, and what kind of habitat they preferred. He experimented with casting distance and practiced casting into a bucket for hours in front of the house. He got so into all this that a friend of ours, a naturalist with a degree in Fisheries hired him to provide worms and perch filets to feed his fish and turtle specimens. In return, he gave Steve a large, fully equipped twenty-gallon aquarium of his own. Once, in a workshop with the curator of the University

Life Sciences Museum, the boys learned how to seine the river to gather fish specimens in a large net. As often happens with unschooled kids who have the chance to immerse themselves in a subject, Steve wowed the fellow with his in-depth knowledge.

None of the boys were immune to fishing fever. All of them, including three-year-old Chris, were happiest when practicing casting, repairing their fishing rods and reels, rummaging through the boxes of lures and sinkers that their Grandpa had given them, and studying angling techniques. The *World Book* was mined for every bit of information they could find. Shaman found an old *Childcraft* book with a section on fly-tying, and proceeded with fishhooks, feathers, wire, and my embroidery thread to construct his own tackle, much of which turned out to be useable. He made lots of illustrated books about fish: *Scavenger Fish, Local Fish, Fresh Water Fish, Ocean Fish*. He made Fish coloring books for Räm and cut out accurate representations of various fish, put paper clips on them, and made a fishing pole out of a wooden dowel, fishing line, and a magnet for Chris. A crowning achievement was his own *Dictionary of Fish*, typed and compiled alphabetically starting with Bowfish and ending with Trout.

The temptation to expand our carnivorous horizons was great when we were offered a rabbit hutch and a pregnant doe. Having not yet built a chicken house that would protect a flock from the coyotes and occasional bobcats, we figured rabbits would be a reasonable beginning to animal husbandry. They were small, could be easily contained in hutches (not quite true, as it turned out), and best of all, would provide magnificent organic fertilizer for my lush raised-bed garden. The younger kids had long been fascinated with rabbits. Ram and Chris and Shaman never tired of building themselves rabbit dens with tables and blankets, which proved to be a useful way to get raw vegetables into them. They often requested salad immediately after breakfast, and once ate an entire pound of carrots in a morning's play. Shaman spent the better part of two months writing and illustrating an epic book about a rabbit who found a giant carrot and got chased by a wolf, which he gave Räm for Christmas that year. All this led me to believe that raising real live rabbits would be an area of high interest as well as a fine opportunity to practice the chores of feeding and care.

Rumors concerning the tendency of rabbits to multiply rapidly are not exaggerated. We were very soon in the position of having to build a rabbit apartment complex. We capitalized on the learning inherent in such a task, reading up on rabbit housing, figuring out how many square feet of cage would be required, and then the actual building of the cages, yet another skill that my do-it-yourself husband surprised me with. The boys were kept busy gathering garden scraps for the bunnies, keeping the cages clean, making sure their water wasn't frozen in the winter, keeping the snow out of the cages, preparing newspaper scraps for nests and innumerable other tasks.

Despite our best efforts and good strong cages, we often had to deal with an escaped rabbit. We spent countless hours scanning the overgrown meadow with binoculars for the telltale rippling of grass, and when we spotted an escapee, Steve took off running after it. He was the only one of us who could catch them consistently, and he still has the scars on his hands to prove it. On some mornings when he had spent a couple of hot hours chasing a rabbit, I seriously questioned not only our lifestyle, but also the decision to unschool. Was this why we were embarked on a radical educational experiment? So my son could chase escaped bunnies in the torrid Oklahoma heat while his age mates practiced their geometry and learned to diagram sentences in climate-controlled buildings?

To be sure, some aspects of the endeavor did present opportunities for in-depth inquiry. Breeding, for example: *Why is the boy rabbit sniffing the girl and hopping all around her? Why is she running around the cage and trying to get away from him? What is he jumping up on her for? Why are they fighting? How come the boy rabbit squealed and then passed out?* Birthing, or kindling as they say in the rabbit world, presented a whole new set of learning experiences. For one thing, it had not occurred to me that occasionally a dam—that's a mother in rabbit-talk—might eat one or all of an entire litter. This really grossed me out and was difficult to explain to the younger ones. Little Chris, looking at me suspiciously: *Do other mothers eat their babies?* We did have a fair share of successful litters, however, enough to keep us building cages pretty consistently.

One late December day, we spent the morning on a Christmas tree hunt in the woods. We found just the right one, a cedar with nice thick branches among a stand of trees that needed to be thinned out. Steve, who at eleven had mastered the axe, chopped it down and dragged it home. We decorated the tree with our motley collection of handmade ornaments, made Castilian hot chocolate, and baked Christmas cookies and gingerbread men for our annual holiday party the next night. Steve practiced a puppet play for the party, Shaman made paper snowflake decorations, and they both perfected card, dice, and magic tricks to entertain our guests.

Amidst the preparations, we discovered that one of our rabbit does had given birth to a litter—six kids, and two of them stillborn. We quickly enlisted the kids in wrapping her outdoor cage in plastic to keep the new ones warm. Shaman was absolutely fascinated with the ones that didn't make it and begged to dissect them. How could I refuse? He and Steve had attended a workshop at a local college with an entomology professor who had taught them to dissect giant, four-inch-long grasshoppers. He had immersed himself in the study of anatomy for months, making all sorts of drawings and models of internal body systems of humans, fish, and other animals, and had recently purchased a book at the science museum on dissection. It was clearly an intellectual pursuit, not just a little boy's enthrallment with blood and guts. I swallowed my squeamishness and agreed to the operation. He scavenged up all the paraphernalia of a sterile dissection and arranged it on a clean white towel: rubber gloves, plastic pan, tweezers, sharp scissors, X-Acto blade, flashlight, and magnifying glass. With

Deck the Halls playing softly in the background, he opened up the tiny creature and laid the various parts out on the towel, excitedly naming everything as he removed it. It was all there—blood vessels, musculature, rib cage, stomach, large and small intestines (he precisely measured these), lungs, heart, esophagus, and liver. He even named the various bones. The pinnacle of the activity was removing the eye from the socket and discovering the clear lens-like eyeball, then peeking through to the brain. He explained to the rest of us how the brain is what sees, as a result of a nerve that leads from the eye to the brain. I somehow managed to transcend my squeamishness to appreciate the excitement of the moment and wondered if a career as a surgeon was in the cards.

Premed training aside, I had a terrible time with the whole rabbit project. I really appreciated the bounteous fertilizer, but I just couldn't bring myself to cook and eat the sweet, furry little creatures without suffering an ache in my solar plexus. I abandoned all rabbit-related tasks to Earl and the boys. To this day, I'm a total hypocrite about meat eating. I do consume the occasional fish or fowl, but if I had to kill it myself I would be an uncompromising vegetarian. And I cannot bear the thought of cooking or eating rabbit, though they are considered quite a delicacy in my Italian Brooklyn neighborhood. I had to face the fact I was not temperamentally suited to animal husbandry and was not likely to succeed at it. But I hadn't given up completely—yet.

We were fed up with the ticks and chiggers that populated our little piece of Paradise. Each night entailed a ritual of checking through everyone's hair for the nasty bloodsuckers. We often had to singe one with a hot match end and pull it out with tweezers. Gross, gross, gross. Plus, we had already had a number of copperheads in and around our house and I lived in fear that one of the boys would get bit. A flock of guinea hens would help solve these problems. These cute little black and white polka-dotted African fowl would eat every insect in sight, and according to local lore, would screech and holler if a snake came anywhere near the house.

There was a very small chicken hut on the land that had been built years ago by some settler, and with a bit of fixing up, it would provide adequate shelter for a few hens, who were much hardier and had better defenses than domestic chickens. We started with some small chicks and put them out in the hut. One day, Steve and I heard squawking and went to see what was up. An enormous blacksnake reared up when I opened the door and stared right at me, like in one of those Indian snake-charmer pictures. One little fowl was a good few inches down his gullet and he had another in his mouth. I was pissed. I grabbed a hoe and swung it at him and he promptly coughed up one little hen and slithered off with the other half digested. We ended up having to bring the rest of the brood indoors until they were mature enough not to get eaten by wild creatures.

The grown hens did indeed eat their weight in insects many times over. But they proved to be very badly behaved. Unlike what the county extension office literature said, they did not return home to roost every night, and once again, Steve was sent on animal-chasing missions, down to some adjoining land where they liked to migrate. He and our dog Benson would chase the flock back to our property. Sometimes they did stay home like good birds should, but instead of going in their house, they would roost up in the cedar trees and party all night. And do they squawk. Eventually these free-range creatures wandered off for good, reinforcing my suspicion that we were not cut out for the animal-raising aspect of modern homesteading.

In the end, literature conquered animal husbandry. We phased out the edible rabbit production and stuck with chinchilla show rabbits after Steve and Shaman got hold of a copy of *Watership Down*, an epic novel about a group of rabbits who escape the destruction of their warren and travel to find a new home, experiencing many dangers and tribulations. These rabbits have distinctive personalities, speak their own language, and have a culture rich with poetry and myth. The allegorical story is informed by the great destructive forces of the twentieth century—the world wars, fascism, totalitarianism— and it captured the imaginations of the boys like no other book they had yet read. Shaman spent many days rendering the book visually, creating a series of drawings that included cross sections of the underground rabbit warrens and the battles that took place. On many of them, he drew grids with all twenty-five rabbits—Hazel, Fiver, Bigwig, Dandelion, and the rest of their comrades—named in a corresponding code. And he has been a committed vegetarian for most of his life.

Steve and I spoke recently over a glass of scotch, in his home overlooking a Norwegian fjord.

"*Watership Down* changed my life," he said. "It set me on the path of an idea that it's an imperfect world, but one in which you have the power to make moral choices."

"Did you have trouble eating rabbits after reading the book?" I asked.

"It wasn't just the question of eating meat," he mused. "But those rabbits in *Watership Down*, they were so personalized. It got me thinking at a very deep level about the nature of good and evil. And, yeh, I never saw rabbits in quite the same way again."

We spoke as well of our pitiful attempts at animal husbandry.

"It wasn't so much that we were bad farmers," he said. "It's just that we were better scientists."

And then he went on to recall fondly their many natural-science experiments with creatures. Indeed, my journals are filled with such stories: the in-depth, extensive study of fish; days of bird watching and identification, observing their flight patterns and what they ate, then drawing them and reading up on their characteristics; collecting lizards, feeding them ants, then watching them shed their skins; hours of observing red ant colonies; digging up and studying the large variety of earthworms on the property; making plaster castings of animal tracks; and finally the frog and toad farm.

As it turned out, we were successful at one animal-raising venture. It began when Steve took a hike to a local pond with Benson.

He discovered scores of mating toads and brought some of them home in a jar—still attached, how exciting can life be? He put them in Chris's little outdoor wading pool and wow! We got to watch a female lay her eggs while the male was still mounted on her. Steve also had brought home a lot of other eggs and some polliwogs, which promptly took up residence in the pool. The next day he and Shaman went back to the pond for more eggs and scored a giant polliwog with the legs already forming and a granddad of a bullfrog. We spent the next few days reading and talking about frogs and toads, their reproductive cycles, what they eat, what part they play in an ecosystem, etc. Steve studied up on identifying all the different eggs and learned that we would soon be seeing some spotted salamanders! In about a week the polliwogs and salamanders hatched out and thrived in the wading pool, providing endless opportunities for measuring, comparing, graphing, charting, drawing, writing, etc. So, yes, Steve was right – we may not have been the best of farmers, but when it came to animal husbandry, we proved triumphant with amphibians.

9 Process vs. Product

"It is nothing short of a miracle that modern methods of instruction have not yet entirely strangled the holy curiosity of inquiry."

~ Albert Einstein

ON MY WAY TO the post office the other day, a mother and her son, whom I guessed to be about seven years old, walked behind me. They were discussing a school project that he needed to complete that weekend. An inveterate eavesdropper, especially when it comes to conversations between parents and children, I slowed my pace to match theirs and took careful note of the conversation.

Mom: It's a life-cycle project. Do you know what the life cycle is? It's the beginning and the ending of life.

Kid: Yeh, like when a butterfly...

Mom: It needs to be in three panels, folded over.

Kid: Like when something is born and when something dies.

Mom: You could do kittens.

Kid: Hmmh...

Mom: Like, the first panel. You could talk about how many kittens are usually born in a litter.

Kid: Or I could...

Mom: Then you could talk about what kittens do and what they eat...

Kid: Yeh.

Mom: and how they grow.

Kid: Okay.

I bet this second grader turned in an "A" project that Monday. Carefully supervised from beginning to end, it likely met all the specifications for a booklet with drawings that matched text and demonstrated that this student understood something about the life cycle. Or at least something about kittens.

But what was actually learned? Curriculum scholars talk about intended and unintended consequences. The intended consequence here, at least on the part of the well-meaning parent, was that the child would create and submit a superior product so that his academic success will be ensured. The unintended consequences, unfortunately, are many: the child's emergent thinking about a big idea was interrupted, and thus compromised; he learned that his ideas don't have merit, or at least as much merit as those of grown-ups; and he has learned that the end *product* is so much more important than the learning *process* that it is better to have someone with more knowledge and skill do it for you.

One could dismiss this anecdote as an example of the contemporary epidemic of overparenting. However, teachers, in their eagerness to show good products, are just as culpable as worried parents. That's why preschool teachers cut out designs for kids to glue rather than let them mess about with little scissors and why junior high teachers only display polished essays on the bulletin board. They know that their teaching will be judged primarily on the end products that their students produce. Unfortunately, this is also why there is widespread plagiarism on the part of students— they have been taught to value the production of a product that meets quality control specifications over the often messy process of learning. Sound like a factory? That's no accident.

Lest I sound like I am casting the first stone, let me confess my own sins. Only a few years ago, I helped Chris, an undergraduate at the time, proofread his essays, and struggled not to rearrange his sentences in more grammatically sophisticated ways. The desire for our children to succeed, to be "accomplished," is a powerful one, all the more in our highly competitive society in which a point or two on a score can make all the difference in the opportunities open to young people. Happily, when unschooling, we had no one looking over our shoulders to approve or disapprove of our products and I was mostly able to able to put my inner editor and my inner supervisor to rest, and focus on the happy surprises that emerged when I simply watched to see where "processes" might lead.

Beginning in 1983 when he was six years old, and intensifying in the next year, Shaman delved into a study of the anatomy of living creatures, including everything from insects to humans. My first inkling of this interest was in September, when he asked me what makes blood red. A friend of ours who was a scientist had gifted us with a marvelous book on the human body that included overlay transparencies of the various anatomical systems, so we got it out and read about the circulatory system. After I read to him, he continued looking at the book. Throughout that year I recorded other of his seemingly casual encounters with the subject: watching a NOVA special on TV about the human body, reading books about Leonardo da Vinci and studying his anatomical drawings. However, the day that he performed whale surgery, I knew something important was going on.

He began in the morning gluing toothpicks carefully together to create the bone structure of a whale. Now, I don't know how much you know about the skeleton of a whale, but I learned some interesting things that day. I learned that whales evolved from land dwelling animals millions of years ago, and that the skeletal structures of some whales still have traces of hind legs. Their front flippers look like short arms with big hands, and they have a whole bunch of extra vertebrae down at the base of their spine where their tails begin. They have vertebrae at their neck just like us humans, but theirs are so "squashed" that they cannot turn their heads, like we do. Their rib cages however, are, unlike ours, extremely flexible. Well and good. It is quite reasonable for a young child to build a model of something he is interested in. He then proceeded to mold the form of a whale around the skeletal structure with some of Chris's homemade, peppermint scented play dough. It was a very nice whale, although to my grown up rational mind, it seemed like all the painstaking work on the skeleton was for naught, as it was completely covered up by the play dough. I had to remind myself that he really did get to know the whale from the inside out.

I was a bit taken aback by what next transpired. Upon completion of the sculpture, Shaman began to make careful incisions with an X-Acto blade to perform surgery on the creature and just as carefully sewed up the incisions with a needle and thread. In my journal, I commented that this seemed to be a "bizarre activity." From a psychoanalytic perspective, it would have been understandable had he or any of the rest of the family been to the hospital for an operation. Cutting a clay creature open and stitching him or her up would be a perfectly reasonable way to work through the visceral fears of being cut open, worked on, and sewed up. But we hadn't had any operations in the family, nor had anyone he knew been to the hospital. Far from an isolated and quirky project, this play-dough surgery prefigured a deep and clinical interest in the innards of living things that would persist through the next year.

A favorite activity was the making of life-size human figures out of newsprint and gluing construction-paper cutouts of the organs onto the human form. Once he spent much of a day on a model of the human body that would never have made it into a science fair or onto a Parent's Night bulletin board. This model consisted of numerous layers: first, the newsprint form, for which Räm donated his body for tracing, then construction paper organs, then a skeleton carefully drawn with Elmer's white glue. So far, so good. But things got really sloppy when he decided to make a realistic circulatory system with red-dyed Karo syrup and wanted the blood to *flow!* He struggled for the longest time to figure out a way to make realistic veins, experimenting with straws and a dropper from a tincture bottle. That design problem was not really solved to his satisfaction and the end product was a horrendous mess. But he had the opportunity to work out, in these and in subsequent similar models, lots of big science ideas having to do with the placement of body parts, the relationships between different body systems, and the important association between structure and function.

Learning is an incredibly complicated process. We have learned more from neuro and cognitive science about how the brain works and what constitutes optimum learning environments in the past few years than in the whole of human history. We know that human beings are meaning-seeking creatures. Out of the bombardment of available stimuli, we select those perceptions that are loaded with meaning or emotional content. In order to make sense out of our perceptions, there must be some previously stored patterns of information that connect to the new stimuli. A pattern of information can be a recognizable object (if one has seen and named a rose, one is more apt to comprehend a geranium), or a familiar series of actions (once one knows "roller skating," "ice-skating" is more easily comprehended). Structures provide patterns for learning ("Once upon a time…") as do relationships (a child's first art is often Big Daddy, Middle-Sized Mommy, and Me). Characteristics and properties constitute patterns (as in "pink" or "round") as do systems (as in heart, lungs, veins, and red Karo syrup). And of course, going up the knowledge hierarchy, the disciplines, whether mathematics, logic, or the study of history, are all based on understanding fundamental patterns and building upon these. The brain is a very efficient connection-making machine. If the school curriculum is filled with content that carries no inherent meaning to students, and if kids do not have the appropriate neural networks (constructed from past experiences) for this content to "hook" onto, then even the most thoughtful and well constructed lessons will fly right by without making a landing. In a class of students, it is unlikely that any given content will hold meaning for all the students, or that they will all have the necessary background knowledge to absorb it. But an unschooled child, with choices about what they learn, will determine for him or herself what to pay attention to, and these choices will be largely determined by their brain's eagerness to absorb this information.

We know that the brain processes information most effectively when it is gained through "immersion" experiences—experiences that involve the whole body, the full range of senses, and the emotions, as well as things like Elmer's glue and red-dyed Karo syrup. Secondhand information in the form of models and pictures is less easily accessed, and information gleaned through symbols (language and math) is last in line, in terms of effectiveness. Despite the commitment of some educators to offer "hands-on" experiences, in truth this is severely limited in all but the most enlightened schools largely because of a misguided need to "cover the curriculum" and cram in as many factoids as possible before the next high-stakes test.

Schools reward the student who sits still, complies with instructions, and passively absorbs what the teacher doles out. Truth is, the system as designed can't cope with the movers and the shakers and the drummers and the dancers, even though we know that lots of physical movement is essential to optimum brain functioning. In terms of efficiency, the unschooler who gets to run around and ride their bicycle as much as they want probably learns as much in a few minutes of focused study as the immobile student who goes home exhausted from sitting all day. There are reasons why humans have developed brains and trees have not. Trees are stationary. We have legs. Our legs and our fingers and thumbs have served the evolution of the human brain for over four million years and there's no reason to think that this relationship is over now.

We know that the brain requires time to process information and that repetition and practice are necessary to embed the new knowledge in long-term memory, where it can serve our needs as a guide to future experience, or as "schema" for the input of new information. Shaman made similar models of the human body over and over again, in spite of the fact that the first or second product might have served as an indication that he had a grasp of the subject. In school, this project, if carried out at all, would have been a one-time event. But for him, it was a process that needed to be repeated endlessly, with minor alterations. The time needed to process information varies from person to person, as does the necessary amount of practice and repetition. This is why a standard pacing calendar is so detrimental to the learning of so many children; it simply cannot accommodate these variations in the time needed to process and practice information. Even the "quick learners," who may be adept at storing information in their short-term memory bank, often fail to retain information or to apply it in new situations if they have not had adequate processing time. Unschoolers not only choose the experiences they want, they determine how much time they need for practice. This is why Shaman (who admittedly fell into the "quick learner" category) needed to make multiple models of the human body. And it's why he drew over two hundred maps, almost daily the year before, and how his knowledge of geography got so embedded in long-term memory that he won a geography contest five years later despite not paying a bit of attention to geography in the interim.

Learning is a social thing, and cognitive research confirms that much learning takes place through conversation and interaction with other human beings. Conventional thinking might assume that kids who are learning without schooling have more limited interactions than their schooled peers. However, in school, interactions are carefully monitored—sometimes there is group work, in which kids get to interact with each other, or "accountable talk time" during which kids can turn to their neighbor for a few moments and discuss prescribed material. Occasionally, they get to ask a question of a teacher, but there is not time for too many questions. The research on unschoolers suggests that they not only have a wider range of social interactions with people of varying age groups, they have vastly more in-depth verbal interactions with knowledgeable adults. With attentive adults, unschooled kids can initiate and sustain conversations that simply would not be possible in a setting with up to forty children and one or two adults. I'd say a good third of what we did when unschooling was to talk. Talk, talk, and more talk. We solved so many intellectual problems—about the origin of the universe, the reason the sun rises, and how babies are born— on that eight-mile stretch of dirt road between Paradise and town. I fine-tuned the art of questioning. There's a reason why Socrates is still synonymous with inquiry-based learning. He was the prophet of the lesson-plan-less learning experience, asking probing, open-ended questions that attempted to get to the heart of the beliefs and ideas that people held, in an effort to get them to question the very source of their understandings. Of course, there is also a reason why Socrates was murdered by the powers-that-be. Too many questions make people in authority nervous.

Our contemporary schools are based on a model that is close to two hundred years old. In the past few decades, almost every social institution in modern society has changed radically—except schools. We have gotten rid of the dunce cap and the switch and the notched board that Earl was beat with so often in his childhood, though corporal punishment in schools is still legal in nineteen states. We now have chairs at tables instead of desks in rows, but we still have prescribed periods of learning punctuated by ear-shattering bells in most schools (just like the ones that summoned folks to work and marked the end of shifts in factories). And despite the presence of silicon-based information machines in most children's pockets, knowledge in schools is still dispensed in prescribed doses by authority figures and everybody still is expected to learn the same thing at the same time, all the better to ensure social stability through a "common" curriculum. If anything, the curriculum has gotten more rigid, with many teachers forced to read from scripts rather than teach in ways that might actually engage the kids, and with more and more high-stakes tests every year to determine people's slot in the educational and social hierarchy.

One is justified in asking why, given all we now know in the twenty-first century about how children learn, education is seemingly locked down in the Industrial Age, stuck in factory-model schools designed in and for the nineteenth century. Unschoolers are harbingers of a radical rethinking of what we think we know about learning, and pointing the way to the remarkable things than can happen when their imaginations are set free, their inventiveness valued, and their potential unleashed. They are a cogent reminder that it is the *process* of learning, in all of its messy, glorious splendor that we should attending to, not just the tidy, polished *products* on the bulletin boards and at the science fairs.

10 The Power of Play

Every child under freedom plays most of the time for years...
~ A.S. Neill

Living is learning and when kids are living fully and ener-
getically and happily they are learning a lot, even if we don't
always know what it is.
~ John Holt

Ah — that is admittedly mystery, thank God, mystery that
keeps play and work neatly divided, although they must merge
for creation. This is the paradox and the reason that play is
the only way the highest intelligence of humankind can unfold.
~ Joseph Chilton Pearce

BEING RESOLUTE ANTIWAR ACTIVISTS, we planned to out-law toy guns. But sometimes I suspected that boys might be hardwired for combat. When Steve was barely two years old, he was very sheltered from the world — no TV set, no movies, no day care, and at that time, not even any little friends to play with. Just a couple of quiet yogis for parents, a Teddy bear, and gentle picture books without a hint of violence in them. When we moved onto our first homestead, the one where we lived in the army tent, he walked into the woods, picked up a small branch shaped like a pistol, pointed it at us, and gleefully said, "Bang, bang, you're dead."

In Paradise, the kids never tired of collecting the perfect branches to whittle into long smooth shafts, attaching these to arrowheads and engaging in hours of competitive spear throwing. A major advance in their combat capacities came with the discovery that acorns made the perfect ammunition for their slingshots. Amazingly, no small birds or wild animals were harmed, nor did they do any permanent injury to each other.

A Window on Paradise, circa 1984
From left to right: Chris, Steven, Räm, Shaman

Once on the way home from town, we discovered a stand of bamboo in an open field and helped ourselves to a few long stalks. Shaman spent the afternoon building a bamboo tipi frame and covering it with a sheet. He moved in, well supplied with books and a pillow and homemade trail mix. Later, bored with munching and reading in his new home, he got the idea to invent a blowgun out of one of the leftover hollow bamboo sticks. He tried loading it with a variety of objects—peanuts, pebbles, straws, and pick-up sticks—competing with himself to see what traveled the farthest. After numerous limp arcs with disappointing ammunition he stumbled upon an amazing discovery. If one duct taped some bird feathers to a pick-up stick, then inserted the dart and blew, the projectile would travel speedily in a nice straight line and destroy one's mortal enemies (or secure dinner)! His excitement probably equaled that of the first human who discovered the physics of the blowgun dart. My contribution here was to mention the poison dart frog, which sent him scurrying to the *World Book*, so I suppose I was complicit in the arms race.

Next to developing advanced weapon systems, nothing satisfied the boys as much as earth-moving: digging canals and trenches and ponds and building bridges and dams in our front yard. This was an inclination, Howard Gardner might call it a "visual-spatial intelligence," undoubtedly inherited from their dad. Raised in the city and the suburbs, my topographical skills consisted of figuring out bus routes and trying different alleys and streets to walk to school. Earl, on the other hand, could speak intelligently about such earthly features as "ridges" and "valleys" and "slopes," plotting in his imagination and with a wave of his arm and a gleam in his eye the best pond sites and the optimum route for a driveway. I would have felt confident escaping from Croatia over the Alps with him during WWII. But that is neither here nor there.

Team Hatley, circa 1986 Räm, Steven, Shaman

Tonka trucks proved useful for transporting and dumping loads of gravel and dirt. Fortunately, we weren't aiming for any *Better Homes and Gardens* landscaping awards. The only contrived aesthetic in the yard was a small circular flowerbed bounded by local sandstone rocks that I diligently guarded from their incursions. I use the word "yard" loosely. There were no clear demarcations like grass or a picket fence on our twenty acres; the "yard" was simply the empty space between our house and the surrounding cedar forest. At any rate, the yard had a slight natural slope, which lent itself to the construction of major fast-running waterways. Shovels and trowels and hands and kitchen spoons served as tools in the redesign of our property. Dams were especially captivating, and experiments in dam building reached a height after reading a book about beavers. They made dams of rocks, dams of red Oklahoma clay, and dams of sticks with leaves stuffed in between. Miniature tipi villages and log-cabin communities sprung up along the rivers. Once, for two entire days, Shaman dug trenches and laid straws end to end, creating an underground water system for a sumac log-cabin settlement.

Occasionally, these engineers would be compelled to test their structures, filling bottles and buckets with water and releasing it in trickles and torrents as they watched what happened to their handiwork. An entire day was spent working out the mechanics of whirlpools with the hose. A summer afternoon downpour would signal that the fun was really about to begin. Out the front door they'd run to test the limits of the systems they'd built, racing against floods to dig yet more tributaries and trenches. I can still see them through the big living-room picture window in their shorts, barefoot, sopping wet, exhilarated, digging with their hands in the red clay to staunch and divert the raging flows of the rivers and streams. Thank goodness researchers have now discovered that dirt is good for the immune system because these boys loved mud. They'd get too dirty to even come inside for a bath and have to be hosed off before I'd let them in the house.

A logical next step after reengineering the earth and creating waterways is to set ships a sailing. Over a period of days, Styrofoam trays, egg and tofu cartons, tongue depressors, scrap fabric, and toilet paper tubes got transformed into barges, towboats, yachts, and sailing ships. More bodies of water—an old tin washtub and Chris's plastic wading pool—were set up. After the boats were built, it was necessary to figure out how to power them. They experimented with making waves of different strengths and frequencies by moving their hands in the water. They blew the boats forward through straws. They dismantled old toys for their battery-operated motors and attached these to the boats. They found propellers from broken balsa wood planes and affixed them with rubber bands. There were boat races and boat battles, whole armadas of invading navies. Often frogs and lizards and grasshoppers became unwitting ship captains and passengers.

If kids have the chance to mess around long enough, sometimes pretty exciting things can happen. We had a box full of weird magnets and had performed lots of different magnetism experiments such as moving a paper clip with a bar magnet through paper, foil, glass, a jar with water in it, and a steel bowl. They had learned how to magnetize sewing needles and spent the better part of one day with a homemade magnet detector, walking around the house looking for hidden magnets. Steve and Shaman had the bright idea to sew a magnetized needle into the sail of a ship, then propel it from a distance with another magnetized needle stuck through a straw. To my astonishment, it worked. I was as excited as the boys were, as would be any teacher or parent who appreciates the power of the process of discovery. I notice that there are now loads of video games to purchase featuring "boat play" but you won't convince me that these can compete with little boys building and sailing their own ships out in the sunshine and the mud and the wind, with live amphibian sailors.

Once, at the end of a particularly thrilling day of inventing and powering boats, I had the bright idea to suggest they write about what they did and what they learned. This benign educational suggestion hit a rock wall of resistance. Hands-down refusal. Put a real damper on things. How could I possibly expect that they could come down from these feverish acts of discovery to *write*? This is about when it dawned on me that there was a critical difference between structured, formal learning and unstructured, informal learning. Unstructured = play. Structured = work. A simple formula, but more often than not, instructive. I began to understand why kids sometimes seem to resist even the most carefully planned and interesting learning experiences, in marked contrast to the inventiveness and total engagement they exhibit when things emerge naturally from their own deeply felt need to discover or express something. I developed a tentative theory I called "Intervention by Invitation." I didn't always live up to it, and had to engage in a fair amount of tongue-biting and hand-sitting, but for the most part, I learned to mostly watch what they did while they worked playfully, or played workfully. Close observation had the added advantage of teaching me when and when not, how and how not, to suggest that they formalize their learning in conventional formats—essays, charts, diagrams, etc. And while I still sometimes wondered if genuine learning was taking place, more often than not their self-initiated play sparked surprisingly sophisticated concepts and conversations about human, environmental, and mechanical interactions.

Once we were reading *The Swiss Family Robinson*, an inspiring classic for young people about how a shipwrecked family survives through their inventiveness on a remote tropical island. We had just finished a chapter where the father uses simple machines such as levers and pulleys to build the family a tree house. The kids were intrigued, so I dug out an essay that described pulleys in more detail, and another on how simple elevator systems work. You could almost watch the boys' brains lighting up as we read, and they couldn't wait to get started trying things out. Shaman rushed to get a discarded milk carton, wire, string, wooden spools, and other detritus and proceeded to construct an elevator. A few less-than-satisfactory attempts and soon he had one that worked beautifully. Younger brothers were always the beneficiaries of such creativity, and that morning, Räm's Star Wars action figures had countless elevator adventures. When delight in elevators declined, Shaman made skis for the action figures out of scotch tape and tongue depressors and poles from shish-ka-bob sticks, and invented a pulley-operated ski lift out of an empty oatmeal carton and string. In such ways, the few commercial toys we did have got repurposed to suit multiple functions.

After lunch, the boys spent the rest of that afternoon outdoors, rigging up ropes as pulleys over tree branches, lifting loads of rocks in buckets and experimenting with lifting boards into trees with pulleys, just like they did in *The Swiss Family Robinson*. Levers and fulcrums made with concrete blocks and old boards sparked similar enthusiastic explorations, hoisting heavy items, making a see saw, and finally, moving various heavy loads around with the wheelbarrow, which is a basic lever and fulcrum system. This lasted until someone, most likely Steve, realized that a truly great capstone experience would be to use all of the available materials—concrete blocks, wheelbarrow, and boards— to construct ramps, and see how far, how fast, and how high they could soar their bicycles through the air with a little help from basic physics. Steve is still basically playing the same game now, twenty-eight years later, on his hand-built fixed-gear bike, and the obstacle course is the boulder-strewn plateau of Norway.

As a girl growing up in the suburban 1950s, I had a fairly gendered play experience: dancing lessons, dolls, lots of books, a record player, and board games. Fortunately, my folks were avid sports fans and my dad sold sporting goods, so I also had the best in basketballs, footballs, baseball gloves, and bats, which I suppose balanced things out. What I never really had, except for a set of Tinker Toys, was either the materials or the encouragement to engage in model building. In the 1950s, model cars and airplanes were for boys only. No surprise that most people who became engineers were men. So as a parent, I was intrigued with how the interest in designing and building developed. One month it would be boats, the next, hang gliders, the next, propellers to power ships and windmills and oil derricks. Sometimes we could afford rocket-ship kits, or some other fancy thing with instructions, but the kids seemed every bit as content to work stuff out with toothpicks, popsicle sticks, glue, aluminum foil, and rubber bands. This play seemed to serve multiple functions: replicating the world they saw around them, building things we read about in books, trying on adult roles, establishing some control over the physical world (all those dams!), or simply figuring out the mechanics of how things worked. I don't think today's kids get enough opportunity to do much of this sort of thing. Most homes aren't quite as abundant in raw materials as ours was, and kids don't have the sheer amount of unstructured time to putter about and follow their inclinations. And such activities do test a parent's tolerance for high levels of chaos. At the end of some days, I would gaze around, paralyzed, at the mess. But living in a construction site was pretty much continuous chaos anyway, so what the boys added hardly made a dent.

School would be a logical place to learn the basics of physics and building and engineering, but there is not a lot of "stuff" to mess around with in schools. Blocks and clay and scrap materials are even disappearing from many kindergarten classrooms now in the frenzy over teaching what can be easily tested. Learning is expected to take place in the brain, not the rest of the body, and with tidy tools such as paper, pencil, and books. I suppose some kids really do learn well this way, though I have my suspicions that the failure to allow for genuine hands-on experiences is at the root of many of our educational problems such as behavioral disruptions and lack of motivation.

Some of the play that went on in our "not-school" would probably have seemed just plain silly to a casual observer. Like the time when I came home from shopping to find that Shaman and Räm had gathered together every stuffed animal in the house and made popsicle-stick and fabric splints and casts for all of their broken, fractured, and sprained legs and arms. They had created an animal hospital out of the large cardboard building blocks and were busy setting up a tri-level concert hall, so the injured animals could enjoy a rock concert. Pretty silly, all right. But if the casual observer were to look under the surface of this outlandish activity, they would learn that Shaman had been immersed in a study of bone fractures for weeks, begun when we had, at his request, looked up "Fractures" in the *World Book* and together studied all the different ways that bones could be broken. Next he had consulted his favored college text on anatomy to clarify some details, and when satisfied, set to work on his collection of accurately labeled pencil drawings of different fractures—simple, compound, transverse, oblique, stress, impacted, and greenstick. These were eventually compiled into a text entitled *My Fracture Book.* To consolidate his knowledge even further, he devised a sort of final exam. He asked me to trace around his body on a large sheet of newsprint, and then he cut out the major parts of the skeletal system from white construction paper and glued them onto his life-sized model. From memory, he illustrated the various bones with different kinds of fractures using correct terminology like radius and ulna and femur and tibia. Honestly, the things these kids thought up to do astounded me sometimes. This test would satisfy any educator that he had "learned" the material, but he still needed to do more with it. He did not know, consciously, that the brain best retains what it learns when you teach it to someone else, but he instinctively sought out a playful experience that would allow him not only an opportunity to practice his doctoring skills, but to share his considerable new knowledge with his younger brothers, who got a kick out of learning and using words like femur and tibia. The multiage learning environment allowed my preschool boys access to activities and ways of thinking way beyond the scope of even the best early childhood classrooms.

While the natural world and found materials constituted the bulk of our educational supplies, we did occasionally have the cash to buy some stuff. I depended on the Edmund Scientifics catalog and learned a lot about science terminology just from reading it. One could spend a fortune with them on solar-powered rainbow makers and crystal growing kits and remote-controlled flying sharks, but we stuck with the basics: magnifying glasses, magnets, electronics boards for making things like alarm clocks and transistors and diodes, and a stopwatch, which got more use than most of our other supplies combined. As in clocking airtime in bicycle jumps off of ramps and timing dam-busting water flows. With the advent of homeschooling, the array of available educational materials has proliferated. Lots of it is junk, but parents are spending enormous amounts of money on everything from infant flash cards to chemistry sets in hopes of improving their children's IQs.

I was seduced by the colorful math toys in the educational catalogs. I loved arithmetic in elementary school, as I had a speedy brain and a good memory. I won timed contests that determined who could do the most correct multiplication problems and was hands-down winner of flash-card games. I even liked word problems, but I had learned all this by rote. By high school, I lost interest because it seemed like nothing but endless droning lectures, diagrams on the chalkboard, and tests. I barely passed geometry, and like about 40% of the rest of the population, spent years thinking, "I'm no good at math." I was determined that my kids would learn to love the subject. We would explore math and music, math and art, and math and life. So, in addition to emeralds and rubies and sapphires, we acquired some conventional math manipulatives. Colorful objects that encourage a hands-on approach to math, thus inviting kids with varying learning styles—kinesthetic, visual/spatial— into the community of math learners. I especially liked pattern blocks—colorful wooden hexagons, squares, triangles, trapezoids, parallelograms, and rhombuses—because they resembled quilt pieces, and I was convinced if my sophomore geometry teacher had mentioned that learning geometry would help me make great quilts, I might have achieved something other than my pathetic grade. I bought Cuisenaire Rods, beautifully colored square rods in centimeter increments, for teaching ratio and proportion. We had Geoboards (peg boards with a zillion rubberbands for teaching area and perimeter), Orbit building straws (kind of a soft plastic Tinker Toy for investigating three-dimensional shapes), and Multi-Link cubes for learning about patterns. Initially, I was excited about the activity cards and worksheets that came with these educational materials. But usually when I tried to arrange a structured learning activity, I met that old rock wall of resistance again. It became painfully obvious to me that free play with materials often resulted in more complex and unpredictable learning than any planned lessons. Not only that, I would often be invited into the free play and end up accomplishing not only the goal I had in mind but much more.

Räm really liked the Multi-Link cubes. I got them out one day thinking we might do some work on more-than and less-than. But he wasn't having anything to do with that idea, and dumped out the carton and set to work making a pistol. I'd gotten over my problem with little boys and their weapons ages ago, so I wasn't fazed. I said, "That's cool," and proceeded to make a replica of his gun. Suddenly this was a game that he had initiated, and we proceeded to spend a half hour or so taking turns making and replicating patterns, counting the cubes in the patterns, learning new vocabulary, and discovering the basics of area and perimeter. Eventually the math play devolved (or evolved?) into a fantasy about a fire-breathing dragon made of Multi-Links, but in the interim we had achieved far beyond more-than and less-than.

I also figured something else out. The lovely activity cards that come with these materials lead one to believe that there is a one-to-one correspondence between an activity and the acquisition of a specific concept. This is one of the prevailing myths of the "outcomes-assessment culture," and it is one of the misguided ideas that are destroying education. The myth goes like this: Teacher figures out what a student needs to know (only nowadays, it's not even teachers figuring this out, but textbook writers and test makers). Teacher implements learning activity that covers concept and makes explicit what outcome is expected of the student. Grade level standards, for example, read like this: "Students will describe objects in the environment using names of shapes and describe the relative positions of these objects using terms such as top, bottom, up, down, in front of, behind, over, under, and next to." Students are tested on the concept. Class goes on to the next learning objective.

Elegant, efficient (remember Elwood Cubberly's factory school?) and erroneous. Most of what we humans know is gathered in far less linear ways, through repeated exposure to things and ideas in the environment. Take that grade-level standard above. No kid learns this stuff in a lesson or two. They learn it through interaction with talkative adults (*Shall we cut your sandwich into triangles? Or rectangles?*) and through frequent prepositional references (*Let's look under the bed for your ball. Look at that big round moon up in the sky! I wonder what that star just to the right of it is called?*). That's informal learning, and it is at the heart of what happens when kids play and when they interact with interested adults.

Play is freely chosen. Play is pleasurable. Play is engaging, engrossing, spontaneous, imaginative, self-directed, experimental, improvisational, purposeful, absorbing, and transformative. It is a negotiation between the inner world of the child and the environment. In play, we try on the world and see how it fits. Isn't this what learning should be all about?

It's not surprising that there are movements afoot to restore free play to its rightful place in children's lives. In recognition that children are spending far more time than is healthy in front of screens, or in highly structured extra-curricular activities such as adult-supervised team sports, a movement has begun to restore children's free play. The movement has a national coalition, annual events in Central Park, and a seventy-five-page booklet that teaches parents how to facilitate such sophisticated experiences as "Climb on the couch with your friends and pretend you are sailing on a ship to a distant land!" Though this is certainly an improvement over kids having their noses buried in a tiny screen or gaining oodles of weight sitting on the couch watching reruns of Sponge Bob, I find it amusing that parents need a manual to facilitate what centuries worth of children have figured out quite nicely on their own.

It's not just kids who are benefitting from this new awareness of the power of play. Management consultants, recognizing that human beings are hardwired for play, now prescribe playful activities for developing creative problem-solving and social skills within a corporation. An intriguing Hungarian researcher named Mihaly Csikszentmihalyi (pronounced *cheek set me hy-ee*) developed a concept he called "flow" or the "flow zone." It's like the state that an artist gets into when painting, or a potter potting—total engagement and immersion in a pleasurable experience. Just like play. Supposedly being in this zone enables the brain to think better and faster, which suggests that if education were to more closely resemble play, it might just be more effective.

11 Passion, Purpose, and Productive Idiosyncrasy

...Great God, I'd rather be
A Pagan, suckled in a creed outworn
So might I, standing on this pleasant lea,
Have glimpses that would make me less forlorn;
Have sight of Proteus rising from the sea
And hear old Triton blow his wreathed horn.
~ *William Wordsworth*

I N THE SAME YEAR that Steve was superinvolved with fish, Shaman discovered the ancient world. He would have been a second grader, had we bought into such conventional ideas as grades. His prior 'year of maps' had led him to an interest in astronomy, and we were fortunate that a close friend and fellow unschooling parent was an amateur astronomer. All of us spent many evenings star-gazing through a high-quality telescope at her house. Learning about the constellations led naturally to reading numerous associated myths and legends. Shaman was fascinated with Perseus and Andromeda, Hercules and the Hydra, and enthralled with the adventures of Jason and the Golden Fleece. Our readings of these epic stories found expression in well over a hundred drawings of legendary heroes and knights and dragons and battles and swords that soon competed for space with maps on the raw sheetrock and stud walls of our perpetual house-in-progress.

His interest in the ancient world really picked up steam the next year, when he would have been in the third grade. One Thursday in October, we played a board game called *By Jove*, which was based on Greek and Roman mythology. He read the booklet of myths that came with the game and was so engrossed in it that I dug out three more books of myths from my library, including the classic edition of *Bullfinches Mythology* and Edith Hamilton's *Mythology*, which he commenced to devour. We had a great conversation that day about the place of myth in classical music, literature, poetry, and fine art. We talked about how cultures all over the world had evolved similar myths. We even got into a discussion comparing Pandora's Box to the Adam and Eve story, and I pointed out to him the ways in which both myths held women responsible for evil in the world. Aha, a teachable moment! Being the good feminist mother of four boys that I was, I was eager to present my hypothesis that such myths might represent the patriarchal challenge to the magic and mystery of the matriarchal societies that existed in ancient times. Heady stuff!

From this day on for the next few months, his bed became a clutter of books, typewriter, art supplies, and mythological drawings. (Full disclosure: during our unschooling years, I often let the boys—horror of horrors—stay in bed to read and do work.) In addition to his proliferating drawings, he built dioramas of the Trojan War, wrote and illustrated his own books of the myths, created a huge "tree of the gods" on newsprint showing the lineage of the descendants from Uranus and Gaea, made numerous charts contrasting the Greek gods with their Roman counterparts, and wrote a play featuring mythological characters.

In the course of writing and typing his play over a number of days, he learned— in addition to playwriting format— new spelling words, how to form contractions, and how to hyphenate words when necessary. Such a haphazard approach to learning academic skills is considered heretical by most educators, who believe that skills need to be carefully sequenced to make sure that no one misses anything. But of course, lots of students miss lots of things, even when skills are approached in a comprehensive way—and for a simple reason. Neuroscientists know that the brain resists imposed information that does not relate to its own interests or needs. When we teach academic skills in an isolated way, outside of the context of meaningful subject matter, students are unlikely to retain those skills, or to transfer them to new situations. Here, on the other hand, was a youngster singlemindedly pursuing his own intellectual interests while accumulating all sorts of "basic skills" along the way.

One day, on our weekly visit to the library, I lost track of Shaman while I was with the younger children. I finally discovered him upstairs in the adult section of the library, sitting on a footstool between musty stacks of the classics. He had located a copy of the *Iliad* and read two chapters of it. He brought it home, and in the course of that next year had read the full-length, grown-up versions of the *Odyssey*, the *Iliad*, and the *Aenead* multiple times. When I say multiple, we're talking five-seven times each. By April, he had also devoured a number of Greek plays, including *Ajax, Antigone,* and *Oedipus the King*, by Sophocles, *Iphigenia in Aulis* by Euripedes, *Electra* by Sophocles and Aeschylus, and *Agamemnon* by Aeschylus, and was working his way through *Tales from the Greek Drama,* which retells the plays in story form.

I recite this litany of texts not to impress you with his intellectual prowess (well okay, maybe a little), but to challenge the prevailing assumption that children's reading needs to be carefully monitored to make sure they are reading on the proper level. The operative phrase now is "leveled reading," a phenomenon that grew out of the Reading Recovery movement (an educational intervention that is necessary largely because we pressure children into reading before they are ready and then need to remediate them when they aren't successful). In what I believe is a misguided obsession with making teaching a science, we've become overly concerned with having children read books that are just right—not too easy, not too challenging. I call this the Goldilocks Theory of Reading Instruction (not too hot, not too cold, but *just right*). We have developed categories of reading proficiency—early emergent, upper emergent, early fluency, fluency, and proficiency—as well as multiple systems of leveling books, and God forbid that a child neglect to master one level before ascending to the next. Teachers often use a strategy called the Five-Finger Rule in which a student selects any page from a book and starts reading it with five fingers in the air. Each time he or she comes across a word they do not know, they lower one finger, and... you got it. If all fingers come down in the course of reading one page then they are instructed to return the book for one that is better suited to their level of proficiency. To me, it all seems a bit like gluing corn on letters, and I suspect that had we been overly influenced by the ideas of leveled reading and the Five-Finger Rule, Shaman might have spent his third-grade year on *Frog and Toad Together* rather than the Greek tragedies.

Räm and Chris were the immediate beneficiaries of Shaman's passion for the ancient world. Hours and days and weeks were spent constructing helmets, battle axes, swords, shields, greaves, handmade Greek sandals, and at one point, a reasonable facsimile of chain mail. We invested heavily in wire, aluminum foil, cardboard, scrap wood, and countless rolls of duct tape. I'm quite sure, in fact, that duct tape was our single largest educational expense for the year. Entire mornings were spent designing and creating just the right attire to reenact one of the epic battles. He would dress up his younger brothers and take them out into the woods where he choreographed elaborate enactments of the ancient stories, directing them to climb to the top of this or that rocky hill, to hide in that grove of trees, and then charge into the heat of battle. After lunch, or the next day, they would pick up where they left off, totally immersed in epic dramas. Of course they loved it! This much "play" would be considered a frivolous waste of time in the normal third-grade classroom, where even recess has been eliminated in favor of test preparation. But the many hours, and I mean *many* hours spent drawing, writing plays, constructing dioramas, and directing reenactments of the stories somehow worked to deepen, extend, and clarify the meanings in the texts he was reading.

One day in January of that year, I caved into my insecurities and took the two eldest boys to have their reading abilities assessed. We went to the Oklahoma State University Reading Lab so that they could take the grade-level placement reading tests. I was deliberately low-key and casual about this process, as I did not want either of them to feel performance anxiety in any way. Shaman indicated by his reading level and vocabulary that he should be tested at the eighth-grade level, but did not perform as well as might be expected on the comprehension segment of the test, which involved repeating details of the story back to the examiner in sequence and answering questions about the text. He missed some details and embellished others, calling to mind his kindergarten entrance exam, when, instructed to draw the human figure—to assess whether he knew the requisite number of hands and feet, and where they belonged—he had drawn a human figure in medieval battle armor, complete with a helmet, bow, and arrow. Now, embellishment *could* be seen as an indication of a creative mind. But in the case of his reading comprehension test, it lowered his score. He was extremely upset and angry on the way home because he felt like he didn't do as well as he should have and told me, red-faced with tears welling in his eyes, that he didn't understand that the details had to be repeated back in sequence.

"And the stories were STUPID!"

The experience confirmed my inherent skepticism about the value of testing and diagnosing young children. This was a low-stress, no-stakes experience with a friendly examiner, and it still caused severe distress in a youngster. In schools today, high-stakes examinations can evoke such dread that some testing companies include latex gloves and a ziplock bag in which to insert the test booklets that students vomit on, because officials are well aware of how stressful the tests are to many children. What madness! The day of our diagnostic tests, we went home and spent the afternoon watching a cement mixer pour piers for an addition to the house, baked oatmeal cookies, and watched a movie about

Harriet Tubman. Shaman commenced reading the *Aenead* for the seventh time. We never bothered with testing again.

At a recent family gathering, he and I discussed his memories of that year. He said that the first time or two he read the *Iliad*, the *Odyssey*, and the *Aenead*, he just read, forging through the texts without necessarily understanding all of the words, and sometimes without garnering a lot of meaning. He had not, obviously, been instructed in the Five-Finger Rule. But he was sufficiently gripped with the stories to read them over and over again, expressing the meanings he was extracting through a multitude of artistic forms.

When there are no planned curricula, no lessons, no required learning, and no tests, young people's interests and passions naturally wax and wane. Shaman's learning cycles lasted for nearly a year; when he would have been a first grader, it was geography, as a second grader, anatomy, and as a third grader, the ancient world. This is not to say that he did not do other things during those years. During the ancient-world year, he studied fish, birds, insects, spiders, and worms, practiced reading and writing cursive, made his way through a standard third-grade spelling book, played a lot with math manipulatives, and worked through an advanced fourth-grade math workbook, mastered Book One in the Suzuki violin program, began to read and write music, and practiced knitting, fly-tying, print-making, origami, off-loom weaving, and mask-making. He studied tae kwon do, archery, yoga, played on league baseball and soccer teams, and became a reasonably accomplished cook. He created for himself what we might call a "well-rounded curriculum." But each year, one interest—one *passion*—dominated, and we had the luxury of time to allow it to play itself out.

I'm convinced that children have an innate sense of how to build upon their experiences to further their learning. It's not surprising to me that many kids do not demonstrate this capacity, for we seldom give them the opportunity to structure their own learning, preferring instead to impose curricula designed by experts on them and expecting them to passively accept external demands and perform to set standards. Has anyone thought about the relationship between this approach to learning and the millions of dollars of educational research money we spend trying to figure out how to motivate children to learn?

When set free in a stimulating environment, with interested adults to provide a bit of guidance, children do not just roam aimlessly from one learning experience to another. They engage in "recursive learning" (revisiting concepts and skills at higher and more complex levels) when they have the need to synthesize new knowledge that they are acquiring. Shaman demonstrated this when he integrated his passion of two years earlier—map-making—into his new passion for the ancient world. After one reading of the *Odyssey*, he spent an entire day on a huge, detailed, butcher-paper map of ancient Greece and Troy that depicted numerous alternate routes that Odysseus could have taken on his way home from the Trojan War. Each route was accompanied by an elaborate written explanation of how history might have been changed in each case. This activity rates pretty high on Bloom's Taxonomy (a scale of thinking that shows progression from simpler forms of cognition, such as memory and recall, to more complex levels, such as analysis and application). I doubt if I would have ever come up with such a rich activity had I been planning his curriculum. But children can amaze us with their astounding creativity, if we only provide them with opportunities to do so!

In August of that next summer, ancient Greece and Rome gave way to ancient India, and here we have the spark that lit the fire that would culminate in his current intellectual passions (he is now in his midthirties). A friend of ours who took an interest in Shaman's learning sent him a series of seven books by K.M. Munshi called *Krishnavatara*, a popular adult book series in India that tells the story of the life of the god Krishna. His learning journey then took him from his early fascination with the Greek and Roman gods to Krishna and the pantheon of Hindu gods and goddesses.

Years later, he would major in Asian religions as an undergraduate, and *teach himself* enough Sanskrit to qualify for a graduate school that required the language as an undergraduate major. He completed a doctoral dissertation that explores the development of Hindu goddess cults (painstaking scholarly work that included a critical edition and translation of the *Brahmayamala*, a Sanskrit text preserved in a palm-leaf manuscript of Nepal nearly one thousand years old), was awarded a Ph.D., and is currently a tenured Professor of Religious Studies at a major university.

What might we learn from studying such longitudinal learning patterns of young people who are free to determine the scope and sequence of their own learning? I like to think of Shaman's ancient world story as an example of *productive idiosyncrasy*, a phrase that I learned from Eliot Eisner, an education scholar who believed that education is more an art than a science. Productive idiosyncrasy argues that there is absolutely no need to turn children out of a common educational mold, even if it does make comparisons of them easier. We have become so obsessed with narrow visions of accountability that many schools have eliminated—in kindergarten no less!—recess, dramatic play, art, music, building with blocks, and even rest period in favor of highly structured math and literacy instruction. You won't find a third-grade classroom today where children might spend days (in Shaman's case, *months!*) constructing armor out of aluminum foil, cardboard, and duct tape and reenacting their favorite myths. In fact, many creative teachers have even given up trying to squeeze the traditional class play into the school year, for it is not likely to enhance the children's test scores, which focus on such easily measured outcomes as the recall of facts and the sequence of events in a story, not on intangibles such as art appreciation or creativity or learning to work well with others.

Productive idiosyncrasy challenges the current fixation on common standards, standardized learning, and testable outcomes, arguing instead for multiple forms of instruction and expression, for attention to the "whole" child and their social, emotional, and aesthetic needs, and patience with the varied timetables children have for learning. To any parent, this seems like just plain common sense. Anyone who has ever raised a child understands their absolute uniqueness, their exceptional individuality. Anyone who has raised more than one child knows this even better, as they observe that even siblings are utterly distinct from one another. If we know this, why do we settle for an education that promotes conformity, adherence to rules and expectations, intellectual dependency, and indifference to one's own desires and passions?

Some people truly believe that we can only have a functioning democracy if we have a common curriculum, a shared body of knowledge, and a common set of learning standards, complete with benchmarks and accountability systems. Surely there are some things that everyone should know. But put a hundred great scholars in one room to decide what these things should be and they will debate endlessly. I know this because I have served on panels and commissions loaded with very smart people charged with coming up with answers to such questions as "what do all children need to know in the twenty-first century?" and have witnessed firsthand the complexity of trying to come to agreement.

What is the worst that could happen if we actually embraced productive idiosyncrasy in our educational system? Would we end up with too many scholars of medieval Hinduism? I doubt it. Humans in almost every society have managed to distribute their skills and talents quite nicely. There are always necessities that need to be taken care of. There are buildings to be built, children to be taken care of, computers to be programmed, people to be healed, oceans to be studied, movies to be made, food to be grown, souls to be tended to, songs to be sung, and ancient cultures to understand. There are such a wonderful variety of things to be done that there is no reason why everyone can't dream their dreams and live out their desires. But, you are thinking...we can't *all* follow our bliss. What about those jobs that no one really wants to do? Don't we need an educational system that prepares people for specific roles in our society?

Indeed, this is what we have had for the past hundred-plus years, a system that uses standardized measures to sort, sift, and rank people. Productive idiosyncrasy, on the other hand, is a radical idea, perhaps one more fitting for the twenty-first century. Were we to embrace it in our educational system, humans —that means us—all of us—might actually take our destinies into our own hands. We might envision the kind of society we want. We might insist upon only doing what is authentic and what feels ethically right. We might refuse to act against our own interests or to engage in work that is destructive or meaningless. And that might lead to challenging the rules of a society that doesn't make room for the persons we REALLY want to be.

12 What About God?

I live my life in widening circles
that reach out across the world.
I may not complete this last one
but I give myself to it.

I circle around God, around the primordial tower.
I've been circling for thousands of years
and I still don't know: am I a falcon,
a storm, or a great song?

~ *Rainer Maria Rilke*

NO QUESTION ABOUT IT, a majority of homeschoolers choose to educate their own for religious reasons, hoping to pass down their values and beliefs intact, uncontaminated by outside influences. This is understandable, given the hazards of modern society. Kids in school, the argument goes, are likely to pick up all sorts of corrupting behaviors—bad language, sexual experimentation, drug use, and a lack of respect for authority—temptations that lead people off the moral path. Parents want the best for their children, and for some families that means providing shelter within a secure cocoon of belief about how the world works, what is right and what is wrong, and how to live a good life.

Unschoolers, on the other hand, are often doing what they do not for religious reasons, but more philosophical ones, such as a belief in individual freedom or the essential goodness of humans. They tend to worry less about the behaviors their children may pick up in schools and more about the failure to develop critical thinking, intellectual autonomy, and creativity because of the standardization of the curriculum and the overreliance on testing. In between these positions are numerous variations.

Values and beliefs are inextricably linked to both the content and the form of education, that is, the *what is learned* and the *how it is taught*. And so, religious homeschoolers who subscribe to strict religious dogmas tend to employ equally rigid, authoritative approaches to learning, like fill-in-the-blank workbooks with one correct answer, while unschoolers tend to be more exploratory, initiating self-directed activities and pursuing open-ended questions through inquiry. And many families find some equilibrium between these positions, often moving toward the pole of freedom as they observe their children over time and gain confidence in their capacity to make good choices.

All parents, consciously or unconsciously, deal with questions of what to teach their children about spiritual matters. Even parents who ignore the topic completely have made a choice with consequences, for religion is a huge force in our society. The religious fundamentalists and the hardcore atheists have it easy. These polar opposites have both, in their own ways, closed off the possibility of changing their beliefs. Decisions about what to teach their children in terms of the existential questions— *Why are we here? Why is there something rather than nothing? Who made the world?*—are pretty much made for them. *God did it, in six days.* Or, *It's a cosmic accident, a random collision of sub-atomic particles.* Those of us who lack such firm convictions must struggle with questions for which there are no easy answers: Should I raise my child in a church or mosque or synagogue, even if I don't buy into the underlying premises? How can I teach them about ethics and morals without the support of an accepted belief system? These questions are not unique to families who choose to educate their own, but they take on a new urgency given the expanded parenting/teaching role of unschoolers.

Some people believe that without a strong faith, children won't have anything to fall back on when times get tough. Or if you don't teach them *your* values, they'll absorb other, unwholesome values. The way I see it, the need to teach your kid *something*, even if you don't believe it yourself, reflects a kind of lowest-common-denominator vision of human potential, or perhaps a distrust of basic human nature. In my heart, I felt that if we just enveloped our boys in unconditional love, allowed them to explore the world on their own terms, took their questions seriously, and spoke truthfully with them about what we know and what we don't know, that they would turn out to be good people who could determine for themselves what they would believe.

Though I have a healthy skepticism when it comes to dogma, doctrine, and strictures, I am an unrepentant mystic. I perceive the universe in all of its manifestations as something sacred, worthy of my reverence and respect. The most basic physical processes — the delicate unfolding of flowers in spring, the glimmer of sunlight on a mountain lake, the amazing bond I feel with my children—are sources of wonder and delight to me. And I sense that there are mysterious things afoot in the world that all of our science has yet to explain — why, for example, I think of a friend I haven't spoken with for a long time and we simultaneously pick up phones to call each other. Why tornadoes sometimes take down two houses and leave one standing perfectly intact between them. Why prayers are sometimes answered. Why you dream of your baby before he is born and he tells you his name. Perhaps all will be eventually explained by neuroscience or quantum mechanics or coincidence or chaos theory. But for now, what feels intellectually honest to me is a position of open-minded skepticism regarding questions of the spirit. I am a *seeker*, not a *believer*.

I was a first-wave Boomer Baby, born post-WWII to nonreligious parents in California, a sunny land of dreams and freedom and new beginnings. We lived walking distance from Golden Gate Park in San Francisco and most mornings my stay-at-home mom loaded me in my buggy and wheeled me to the Japanese Tea Garden in the heart of the park. I suppose this is where my early love of all things Asian was engendered. Long before the hippies hit the neighborhood, my spirituality compass pointed decidedly eastward. On one of our regular visits to Chinatown, I purchased a small golden Buddha with my saved allowance, set up an altar in my bedroom next to the record player where I listened to *Giselle* and *The Sleeping Beauty* and *The Dave Brubeck Quartet*, and declared my belief in reincarnation. I was eight.

My mother and I were Palm Sunday, Easter, and Christmas Eve churchgoers. My dad never accompanied us, always saying that if he were to walk through the doors, the walls would likely fall down (a sentiment he expressed loudly, when at ninety-six and in the last days of his life the nursing home folks asked if he would like a visit from a priest). But mom took it into her head when I turned twelve that I should be confirmed, so I attended classes for a few weeks in preparation for taking the wine and the wafer. I didn't mind at all, for the occasion warranted a fabulous new dress, a cap-sleeved white-linen sheath sprinkled with tiny embroidered pink and blue flowers. Even more wonderful were the accessories: a pillbox hat with a veil, white cotton gloves with a pearl clasp, one-inch high heels, and nylon stockings. This coming-of-age as a Woman of the Episcopalian Church in San Francisco's Grace Cathedral was presided over by Bishop James Pike, who came to be known as a dangerous radical and something of a heretic for his unorthodox views on reincarnation and psychic phenomena (he co-wrote a book with his third wife, Diane, *The Other Side: An Account of My Experience with Psychic Phenomena*, which narrated his successful efforts to contact the spirit of his deceased son). Bishop Pike got lost in the Judean desert when seeking to retrace the footsteps of the historical Jesus and died there. I never became a regular churchgoer, but I'm convinced the good bishop infused my wafer with his mystical leanings, not to mention the antiracism, feminism, and peacenik sentiments that got him into hot water with the mainstream Church.

I discovered yoga at about fifteen years of age. I suppose the fact that I was a dancer is what drew me to the practice, for like most people who discover yoga, the physical aspect of it — hatha yoga — is what first engaged me. A couple of years later, living on my own in Hollywood and training at the American School of Dance, I happened to be working on a movie set at the old Allied Artists Studios, out on West Sunset Boulevard. The stars of the movie (I was a mere extra) were all passing around a hefty orange book, *Autobiography of a Yogi* by Paramahansa Yogananda, who was one of the earliest emissaries to bring India's wisdom teachings to the US. They invited me to have lunch with them at the nearby Self-Realization Fellowship, a temple founded by Yogananda, and there I ate my first soybean patty and brown rice, and discovered herbal tea. It was a gestalt moment. I bought the book, decided to try vegetarianism, and began a lifelong journey of yoga study, which to my delight turned out to encompass considerably more than a system of exercises for health and well-being. Though I sought teachings from various gurus and teachers in my young life, I looked no further following my initiation by Shrii Shrii Anandamurti in the early 1970s. Though I don't claim to be an exemplary yogi, the daily practice sustains my soul. I have been blessed or cursed (it depends on the day) with an overabundance of what Howard Gardner calls "existential intelligence." Long before the day I brought the golden Buddha home, I was obsessed with those ultimate questions that have no easy answers: *Why are we born? Where do we go when we die?* And the persistent one that used to drive my mom crazy: *How far is infinity?* Given my insatiable existential curiosity, it's not surprising that I was drawn to a spiritual practice with an emphasis on experience and exploration, rather than on dogma.

In contrast to my liberal, laissez-faire spiritual upbringing on the West Coast, Earl was raised in a deeply conservative Southern Baptist church, surrounded by people who were relentless in their insistence that he must be *saved*. The preacher of their small

Oklahoma church had a crew cut and a red face bulging above his necktie, a face that turned a venous shade of crimson as he pounded the pulpit and bellowed about hell and damnation every Sunday morning. One day, he drove up to Earl's house in the latest model Cadillac wearing a plaid sport coat and flashing a large diamond ring, to find out why the obstinate twelve year old had not yet agreed to a baptismal dunking. Earl, who was born with an above-average crap detector, was suspicious of where all that money in the collection basket went, and I suspect that his distrust of capitalism grew hand in hand with his distrust of organized religion. But the social pressure was so persistent that he finally agreed to be dunked. When everyone in your community is in your face about how you haven't been saved and you are going to hell, and besides, you really aren't *one of us* until you've been immersed, well, there's only so much a young man can take. He was open to the possibility that once saved, he would be *born again,* would feel like a new person, and he would share this wonderful feeling and firm conviction that everyone around him seemed to have.

On The Day, Earl sat with his parents through the service, observing the crescendo of facial color that mirrored the vivid descriptions of fiery torments that awaited the unsaved. The difference, he told me years later, was that today everyone kept looking over at him like he was someone special. Gone were the wrinkled brows of concern and the disapproving headshakes, and in their place, tight smiles and knowing nods. When called forward to be dunked, he walked the endless stretch to the oversized bathtub to the strains of *Come home, come home; ye who are weary come home.* He disrobed down to his bathing suit. The preacher, wearing rubber rain boots, stood in the tank, and a circle of church deacons surrounded it. When Earl joined them, shivering yet hopeful of a good outcome, the preacher, in his best fire and brimstone voice, asked him if he had accepted Jesus as his Lord and Savior. When Earl said yes, he lowered him *In the Name of the Father and the Son and the Holy Ghost* with some assistance into the tank.

Later, dried off and saved, he walked outside with his parents. Everyone was full of hugs and joy and congratulations and good wishes and thankful that he'd been cleansed of his twelve-year-old sins. Happy to be accepted—finally—into the group, he then searched his heart for the magical new feeling. And found............. nothing. Nada. He walked away from that service and away from the church, and never returned.

What cosmic forces create those attractions that join people's lives and destinies? This is truly one of the great mysteries. Earl and I traveled very different spiritual paths and life journeys but we were somehow at similar points on the cosmic continuum the moment that we met in front of Flaming Rainbow. Like me, he was a serious practitioner of yoga, having been initiated by Roy Eugene Davis, who was a monk in Yogananda's Self-Realization Fellowship. He had even lived in an ashram for a while prior to our paths crossing. When we were first married, we maintained a regular practice of meditation, up to four hours a day, and we lived on the ashram/farm near Skiatook, Oklahoma for a short time. Until the oversexed billy goat and the copperheads nesting under our front step and Earl's decision to go to graduate school drove us away to the city. When Shiva Kumar arrived, I assumed we would be able to carry on with our disciplined lifestyle, perhaps with minor modifications. To some extent, with a brand-new infant, this worked out. But I had not anticipated the cataclysmic will of a toddler. One morning when I was sitting blissfully in full lotus in front of a flickering candle, this little bundle of energy burst into the meditation room, leapt upon my back, and threw his arms around my neck in a headlock.

"MOMMY! I'm up!"

At that moment, it dawned on me that things were going to be different. Sure, I could squeeze in a quick meditation when he napped, if I didn't fall asleep myself while nursing him, but once Shaman came along, there was no hope. I don't think they ever both napped at the same time. Not once. So, Parent Yoga turned out to be something other than Ashram Yoga. And that was okay. "Householders" could be yogis, the tradition said, the discipline was just a bit looser. I didn't realize at the time just how much looser it would get.

Kids have an amazing way of bringing you down to earth. They are such *embodied* creatures, full of noise and smells and fluids and wants and needs, and everything is just so *immediate*. They are the teeming opposite of the abstract and the contemplative, although they are great gurus of the "Be Here Now" school. Clearly they were not going to integrate quietly into our household ashram but would bring a very earthly energy to it. I think this took us a bit by surprise, but once we adjusted to the new reality, we began to think about how to raise our wonderfully worldly kids to be spiritually aware, ecologically sensitive, compassionate, and mindful human beings.

There were a number of available choices about how to cultivate spiritual character in one's kids. You could be true believers and admit no contradictions. This is often incredibly successful. I am truly impressed, for example, with the many Orthodox Jewish communities in my Brooklyn neighborhood who somehow manage to keep their young in the fold, despite the pervasiveness of popular culture, and with Amish communities that have sustained cultural and religious coherence, not to mention premodern lifestyles, right in the midst of modern culture. On the other hand, folklore is rife with versions of "the preacher's daughter" stories, which suggest that sometimes even with the strictest upbringing, children manage to turn themselves into just the opposite of what their parents would hope for. We could, however, have adopted a belief and stuck with it and allowed for inquiry and questioning. But my studies in comparative religion pretty much ruined me for true belief, and it would have been intolerable to be an imposter. Anyway, the world was so full of intriguing belief systems, how could one possibly choose?

Earl had discarded Christianity but was gradually coming to a deeper understanding of the part of his ancestral spiritual heritage influenced by traditional Cherokee beliefs. These were perfectly consistent with our environmental concerns, and while the Native American worldviews that I am familiar with are rooted in specific cosmologies and fundamental beliefs, they are also characterized by the same open-hearted generosity of spirit that typifies yoga and other contemplative practices. For my part, I kept practicing Parent Yoga whenever I could steal a few minutes and tried to expose the kids to a wide range of ideas about the sacred and the spiritual, and to different creation myths and ethical systems—sort of an elementary comparative-religion curriculum—even at the risk of ruining them for true belief. To satisfy the need for community that a church often fills, we joined the local Unitarian congregation. Kindred spirits, those folks—accepting of all beliefs, committed to a spirit of critical inquiry, and dedicated to living socially responsible, ethical lives. Many of the Unitarian families were university professors who were intrigued with our unschooling experiment, and we ended up creating an educational enrichment cooperative with them that turned out to be a significant feature of our kids' education.

I realized early on that pretty much everything we did, be it freezing insects for close observation or pondering America's role in world affairs, had an ethical or spiritual dimension. My attention turned to figuring out how to infuse whatever learning went on with a sense of the sacred and an engagement with the ethical issues that might arise. Religious homeschoolers have it made in this department— they have all sorts of curricula available that squeeze every conceivable bit of subject matter into a well-wrapped religious package. Science and social studies take on interesting and peculiar characteristics when forced into such containers; one must be able to disregard all evidence to the contrary, for example, to accept ideas like the earth being created a mere six thousand years ago. I got an inside look at these curriculum packages, as we hung out with an eclectic group of local home and unschoolers. In our ever-shifting group was us, with our leftist leanings and

Earl's Native American spirituality and our yoga practice, a committed atheist family whose parents were brilliant physicists and steadfast peace and justice activists, two conservative Mormon families, a Catholic family that grew at a remarkable rate during our acquaintance (eight children at last count), a Wiccan family that lived in a commune down the road, and an assortment of half-hearted Protestants. We spent a lot of time together, but there were some subjects that we tacitly agreed not to broach.

Once we all attended a religious homeschooling convention at Oral Roberts University in Tulsa. There were numerous vendors peddling everything from science textbooks for teaching creationism to phonics workbooks to Bible study kits. Here's where I discovered that homeschooling, if not unschooling, was big business. I was working to keep an open mind, but in perusing the children's picture books, I came across one that to me seemed emblematic in terms of the lengths people will go to revise history and shape the world to their personal ideologies. It was a book entitled *The First Thanksgiving*. One illustration showed industrious Pilgrims in starched collars and knickers and steeple hats building houses, harvesting crops, and women bringing dishes laden with foodstuffs to a long table. Peering through the branches of the trees lurked dark-skinned savages with feathers and face paint. The text read, "If it hadn't been for the Pilgrims, the Indians would have never made it through that first winter." Thank goodness Earl wasn't there that day. He'd have let out a Cherokee war whoop that would have shaken the walls of the conference center.

I'm not picking on Christians, really. I don't happen to know any staunch communists who homeschool, but true believers are true believers, whether it be in the dictatorship of the proletariat or in the six-day creation of the world. How to facilitate learning and cultivate an inclusive spirituality without imposing dogmatic ideas was a central question for me. What I realized is that no matter what I did, there was no escaping the fact that beliefs and values are shaped in small, everyday interactions. This is important for all parents to understand but it becomes crucial when you spend an unusual amount of time as a family. The best we could hope for, I figured, was to be as honest and transparent as possible about what we were doing. When we did experiments with solar collectors and a magnifying glass, I didn't hide my commitment to renewable energy. When we built a compost heap and grew an organic garden, it was clear how I felt about chemically produced food. How could we help communicating our desire to be "good stewards" of the planet? When we read stories and myths from a variety of cultures and religious traditions, it was obvious that I hoped they would be open-minded and tolerant people who cherish human differences. And so on.

We posed ethical dilemmas, not dire ones like the well-known lifeboat exercise, but simply around everyday things like discussing the pros and cons of animal testing when reading product labels. I wanted my boys to grow up knowing that the small daily decisions they made mattered. The kids didn't get a lot of answers; in the spirit of free inquiry they usually got more questions, because I wanted them to think of themselves as smart people who were already in possession of important knowledge. But sure, I had ideas about the kind of people I wanted them to be, and even if I did make a sincere effort not to brainwash them, they surely got some pretty strong hints about my leanings by the activities I initiated, the conversations I started, and the materials I offered.

People learn to be the kind of human beings they are mostly by watching and mimicking the people around them. It's a long-term process, this parenting business, requiring an inordinate amount of attention to our own behavior and impulses. Yoga proved helpful, with its emphasis on mindfulness and metacognition, or the art of watching yourself think and monitoring your reactions. Practicing the daily discipline of patience and just noticing whatever was happening without rushing to intervene, or scold, or correct, or take action, was incredibly helpful when in the day in/day out company of a rambunctious group of little boys. Which is not to say we didn't lose it now and then. There were those rainy days when the walls would echo with their indoor bickering and I couldn't boot them out the front door, or times when we needed to be somewhere and it was like herding kittens to get them into the truck, and I would shout, "Okay! Democracy's OVER!" But we managed to be more or less consistent, mindful of the fact that the environment, the relationships, and the emotional climate were probably more important than any lessons on character or values ever could be. And our connections with an international yoga association brought a steady stream of crimson-robed monks to our home when they came to our region to lecture or teach meditation. In terms of spiritual role models, they were the best. They were serious and disciplined about their meditation practice, and gave the older boys personal lessons in meditation and the spiritual life. But best of all, they invariably had a great sense of humor and played soccer and Frisbee with the kids, taught them martial arts, and took them canoeing. Chris was convinced they were ninjas.

God does not really come up naturally in the course of children's inquiries, unless they hear a lot of God-talk around them and get curious. Transcendence, which is at the core of most religions, really is an adult pursuit. Children are busy constructing a self and not generally interested in rising above it or getting beyond it. But they certainly do ask Big Questions: *Where did I come from? How did I get here? Why are there stars? Why do people die? Are there people on other planets?* And *how far is infinity, Mom?* They are filled, in a way that we grown-ups might have forgotten, with the mystery and the magnitude of what it means to be alive. Their senses are awake and quivering and the world in its newness appears an enchanted place, with dragons in the clouds and trolls in the trees. In the end, I realized it is not about how to create a spiritual curriculum, or how to teach lessons in ethics and values, but simply about *being fully in the presence of children*, noticing what they are seeing and hearing and touching and smelling, and appreciating the opportunity to share in their perceptual world.

It's about paying attention to the miraculous way that language emerges and thinking develops. It's about accompanying them on their discoveries and rediscovering the extraordinariness of the commonplace things in nature — a grasshopper's jaws, a lizard's detachable tail, a dirt dauber's architecture, or the metamorphosis of a caterpillar into a butterfly. It's about *coming to our senses*, remembering what it means to be alive, awake, perceptive, curious. Meditation, contemplation, and mindfulness training are designed, after all, to get us back to these states of mind—openness, wonder, awe, appreciation—that children dwell in naturally. Unschooling, when you manage to get past conventional ideas of teacher and student and lessons and learning, is an incredible opportunity to explore together the magical mysterious world we are born into and ponder the unanswerable existential questions. And be all right with that.

13 Becoming Human

Classroom attendance removes children from the everyday world of Western culture and plunges them into an environment far more primitive, magical, and deadly serious.
~Deschooling Society, *by Ivan Illich*

PICTURE THIS — FOUR boys ages eleven to fourteen holed up in a loft in the early days of the desktop computer, teaching themselves the basics of computer programming, bulletin boards, modems, and light hacking. Spending long days immersed in Dungeons and Dragons, that role-playing game that was accused (and eventually vindicated) of fostering everything from Satanism to schizophrenia to prison gangs. Riveted to the primitive space warfare and fantasy-adventure video games that were available back in the 80's.

Steve and Shaman became best buddies with Rob and Dave, whose family started homeschooling when it became apparent that the intellectual resources at their local school were seriously deficient. To make matters worse, a couple of badly bloodied noses confirmed that the boys would be subject to the regular torture meted out to nerds in a tiny rural Oklahoma town. Their parents, Earl and Barbra, were physicists. He was a tenured professor at the local university who specialized in laser crystals. She was taking time off to tend to the boys and her gigantic iris patch, and to devote countless volunteer hours to the peace and justice work that brought us together. Given that they had a rambling ranch house and we were living like the Joads in *The Grapes of Wrath*, we spent many evenings at their place enjoying Barbra's fine cooking, star gazing through their professional quality telescope, and talking politics, quantum mechanics, UFOs, and other unsolved mysteries of the universe while the older boys battled it out in space upstairs. Their house became a second home to Steve and Shaman. Our boys loved it; after all, we passed our days in 984 unfinished square feet of construction, and Rob and Dave not only had air conditioning and computers, but an unlimited supply of soda pop. When the four of them tired of violent video games and supernatural drama, they would roam the forty acres of pasture and ponds and go fishing or chase cows. Earl and Barbra, with their advanced degrees in chemistry and physics, aided and abetted science experiments that included rocket launches, smoke bombs, stink bombs, pipe bombs, homemade fireworks, experimental chemical explosions, and solar-fire starting. Once during the course of one of their regular fireworks fights Rob shot off a bottle rocket that lodged in Dave's backpack, which happened to include his arsenal of explosives. Dave managed to rip it off and toss it away in time for them to revel in the spectacle of its contents all going off at once. I suppose this was not what most parents would call a "safe space," but did they ever have a blast. Were all this to take place in today's fearful, overprotective climate, the headlines might read "Homeschooled children of left-wing parents in rural Oklahoma study computer hacking, occult mysteries, and bomb building," and we would have become poster families for the social dangers of homeschooling.

There are very good reasons why governments like to run schools. Schooled kids spend roughly 1300 hours a year in classrooms. Add to that three to four hours of nightly homework and commute time and it comes close to 1500 hours a year. That's a lot of time to mold the character and cognition of impressionable children. National governments have a vested interest in creating the types of citizens who will uphold dominant national values. This was true in Fascist Germany, it was true in Communist Russia, and it is true in Capitalist America. Without a shared value system, the thinking goes, what will be the social glue that holds the nation-state together? Many countries mandate that all children be in a public or private school, and some, such as Germany (hearkening back to laws originally implemented by Adolph Hitler in 1938), are busy prosecuting those parents who choose not to send their children to school, in some cases taking their children away. In other countries, unschooling is legal but highly regulated, the regulations most often taking the form of mandated curriculum and/or state exams, which to my mind, doesn't quite qualify as "unschooling." The US, perhaps reflecting its historically skeptical attitude toward centralized, tyrannical authority has relatively liberal laws, making it legal to opt out of schooling in all fifty states, though families are subject to the regulations of those states. The fierceness of the on-going debates over unschooling and homeschooling reflects deep anxieties about social control — with shaping the type of citizen that will best serve our national interests.

The problem of course, is that we have no real shared opinion about what constitutes our national interests or the type of person who might uphold these. The United States is a huge, complex, and pluralistic society and achieving consensus around what kind of adults we want our educational system to produce is a daunting task. People who believe in the exceptionalism of the United States and think we should be the Police of the World support a social studies curriculum that promotes unquestioning patriotism and an unblemished view of our history. Others, who see the US as the perpetrator of genocide, imperialism, and exploitation seek a critical, culturally diverse approach to the study of history. Some people think that schools should focus on job skills that will prepare the next generation to reign supreme in the global economy. Others think that we should be educating young people to be staunch environmentalists who uphold the rights of all species, not just the economic interests of humans. Some folks want our curriculum to reflect Biblical teachings like creationism, others are avowed atheists and support the primacy of logic and science.

These differences are the source of periodic and ferocious culture wars over what should be taught and they are probably why we have a flourishing system of private, public, and parochial schools. And it is probably why we in the US lean in the direction of less regulation of unschooling than much of the developed world. There are just too many competing interests at stake.

Because many homeschoolers are conservative Christians, much of the call for regulation of homeschooling comes from liberals who claim to be worried about the state of our democracy. I, too, am worried about the state of our democracy, but not because of a few parents who choose not to send their kids to school. I am concerned about our democracy because it has become a "corporatocracy," ruled by a wealthy elite and their government collaborators in *their* own interests. I do consider myself a liberal person who values a diverse, open, and tolerant society. I am appalled by people who believe in white supremacy, or who trumpet the superiority of their religion over others, or those who want to turn back the clock on gender roles or believe that gay people should be stoned. I weep for the children of parents who keep their children out of school so that they can inculcate them with such prejudices, and I am alarmed at the fanaticism that more and more frequently rears its ugly head in our society. But if we believe that we need to suppress the rights of those who express intolerant views in our efforts to foster a tolerant and diverse society, then we are soon tangled in a paradoxical thicket. It's a bit like advocating democracy for a conservative Muslim country and then freaking out when the people there vote for an authoritarian religious state. Impossible contradictions. If we believe in liberty, then we must support liberty, even if some free people hold views that are anathema to us, and we must rely on persuasion, not imposition, to create a just and tolerant society that celebrates difference. And trust that the good instincts of humanity just might win the day. In fact, advocates and practitioners of the strictest brand of fundamentalist home-schooling are reaping the natural consequences of their practices as numbers of their children come of age, reject fundamentalism, and establish social media sites like *Homeschoolers Anonymous* and *No Longer Quivering*, which aim to expose the abuse and neglect that can accompany homeschooling. Kids, even those subjected to the most stringent mental conditioning, have the remarkable potential to become free thinkers and questioners.

The average person who worries about homeschooling and unschooling, however, is not so much worried about abstract ideas like citizenship, but with how unschooled children will learn to interact with others and adapt to the larger world outside of the home. How will they ever learn to get along with people who are different than themselves? What's to keep them from becoming social misfits, or worse yet, sociopaths like the Unabomber? How will they fit into society? How will they ever learn to 'tough it out' in the face of (fill in the blanks: academic challenges, bullying, competition, teasing, etc.) What's to prevent parents from passing their narrow-minded biases and radical ideas along? Even if people concede that young people can learn academic content as well or better in the home environment, much of the criticism leveled at unschoolers is about the socialization process, as though schools were the only possible places that young people can learn to be human successfully.

Granted, there are homeschooling families who really *don't* want their children to get along with people who are different than themselves in terms of race, socioeconomics, religion, or sexual preference. They are not particularly interested in their children fitting into society, because they *disapprove* of secular society. And they aren't worried about passing their biases along, because they are quite sure they have cornered the market on the Truth, and they *want* to pass it along, freethinking not being in their repertoire of desired educational outcomes. However, it would be stereotyping to assert that these were general characteristics of all unschoolers, even religious ones. Most home/unschooling parents tend to be very much like other parents in terms of the social skills that they see as valuable: cooperation, communication, friendliness, empathy, sharing, self-control, responsibility, basic good manners, and the ability to get along with diverse others. In a number of research studies, homeschooled and unschooled children rated significantly higher on these measures than the norm and in many other cases there was no difference. Homeschooled children tend to have the same number of close friends as children in other environments, higher self-esteem, and better relationships with significant adults. And some studies have found that homeschooled children are less likely than others to engage in illegal and antisocial behavior as adults.

I was as concerned as the next person about the kind of adults my kids would grow up to be. Like most parents, I wanted them to be healthy, happy, able to form meaningful relationships, possess the skills to earn a living, and participate fully in the life of society. But my view of the "good society," as philosophers say, was far out of the mainstream at the time. Earl and I did not support consumerism and the unlimited-growth economy, we did not support American military adventures abroad, we protested the destruction of the environment, and we didn't even eat the same kind of food that most folks ate. Young parents in the twenty-first century may find it hard to believe that vegetarianism, organic foods, natural childbirth, attachment parenting, and all the other cool lifestyle choices people have now have not been part of the US mainstream for all that long. Back in our day, we were seen as hopelessly out of sync with the general population. We felt a responsibility as parents to raise children who were at least as conscious as we were about the things we felt strongly about, and would not go on as adults to live in unsustainable ways that would perpetuate these large-scale problems. So I admit it; it really all came down to values, and our desire to raise our children in accordance with the things we truly believed in. Like many parents today, we saw the conventional school as a place where kids were socialized to dominant values that we most passionately did not share. What has changed now is that schools, with their nonstop test-prep curriculum and increasingly narrow focus on "college and career-ready skills," are even more harmful to the development of children than they were in the 1980s. At least back then, kids still, for the most part, had recess, music, field trips, drama, sports, and art (except in Paradise Township!) to break up the tedium of the worksheets.

Like many parents today who opt out of school, I worried that our boys would not have enough opportunities for peer interaction, so we probably erred on the side of overscheduling them. I made sure that they would be allowed to play on school sports teams, and every season saw us shuttling back and forth to soccer, baseball, basketball, and martial arts practices, games, and tournaments. While these highly structured activities provided important opportunities for physical exercise, skill development, and socialization to group norms such as teamwork and good sportsmanship, they did not offer a great deal in the way of cultivating friendships or other kinds of socialization. For that, we relied on our ever-changing network of unschoolers, that eclectic array of Mormons, Catholics, Wiccans, atheists, and half-hearted Protestants. The great variety of philosophical, religious, and political beliefs in this group suggests that all unschoolers are not, as common belief would have it, shy of hanging out with diverse others. We tried a number of things as a group: field trips to museums, factories, planetariums, nature preserves. One parent was on the cusp of the computer revolution before the rest of us, and she informally shared what she knew about her Commodore 64 (remember those?). That same family had horses, and everybody got to ride. And of course there was all that bomb building and computer hacking that went on after Steve and Shaman and Rob and Dave hooked up. Much of this interaction was informal and largely unstructured.

Occasionally someone would decide to teach something. Once my Wiccan friend from down the road tried to teach the kids Spanish, and one of the Mormons, a French teacher, attempted to get parents and kids alike going in a French conversational group. Most of these structured activities fell short of the mark. Socialization is really about kids having many opportunities to navigate the nuances of peer interaction: how to share things, communicate effectively, make and follow rules, work through conflicts, etc. And unstructured play, with as little grown-up intervention as possible, is probably the best way for all this to happen. Unfortunately, unstructured play is a rapidly disappearing phenomena, what with the uber-organization of kids' time (I'm sorry, but I find the concept of a play date hilarious), fear-based restrictions on kids roaming the neighborhood or playing in the woods, and the ubiquitous presence of the screen (TV, video games, smart phones) in young people's lives. All these obstacles to genuinely free play mean that some of the vital ingredients in a rich, exploratory childhood are missing.

Schools occasionally try to teach social-emotional intelligence, which is a fancy way of talking about how to help kids get in touch with their feelings and get along with each other. Given the testing frenzy, such fluff is usually neglected now. Instead, there is an interesting form of academic socialization going on, which has little to do with fostering positive peer relationships and everything to do with conditioning kids to dominant practices of academic and corporate cultures. If you read the first chapter of this book (and you can certainly be forgiven for skipping around to only what grabs your fancy) you might recall me talking about the historic purposes of schools, among which was the "Americanization" of all those unruly immigrants. Well, not much has changed. We still have loads of immigrants, not to mention a fairly sizeable underclass that has been well socialized to street culture and fails to see much point in drawing inferences from a nonfiction text or performing operations on vectors. These masses, the thinking goes, must be taught the "language of schooling." Hence, rather than conflict resolution and democratic class meetings (the kinds of activities that actually promote social-emotional intelligence) we now have a focus on "accountable talk," supported by such "scaffolds" as sentence starters ("I disagree with that because....") or "I'd like to add..."), graphic organizers (Venn diagrams, Frayer models, KWL charts, Main Idea and Supporting Details, and other tools for organizing random thoughts), cooperative learning with carefully delineated roles (leader, timekeeper, recorder, etc.) — all forms of carefully managing thinking and managing talk in the interest of learning. In academic lingo, this is called "socializing intelligence," an interesting convergence of the academic and social purposes of schooling. Many kids, especially those who have not been socialized to conventional middle class norms (which tend to be more or less consistent with the norms of schooling), vigorously resist these efforts to modify and control their behavior. So teachers expend an enormous amount of energy getting kids on task, keeping them on task, and otherwise struggling to enforce the rules of the classroom and get them to engage in accountable talk, instead of talking about things they are genuinely interested in.

Now I have no problem with young people learning the languages of power, the coin of the realm that will gain them entry into the hallowed halls of higher education and the professions. It's good to know how to listen to others respectfully, clarify what you think you heard, and learn how to attend carefully and contribute meaningfully to a discussion. I have even taught my teacher education students how to conduct Socratic Seminars, carefully structured forms of group discussion. The problem, of course, is that these formats are not really about stimulating thinking, but about containing and compartmentalizing thinking and managing social behaviors. Unfortunately, children who are successfully "intellectually socialized" find when they get out into the actual world that the exercise of intelligence involves more than being able to write a three-paragraph essay that makes a claim supported by three pieces of evidence, or that professional conversations using sentence starters are not how people in the workplace actually talk.

Even if the bureaucratic attempt to manage language use and behavior in classrooms were to find some level of success, what has not changed about schools since I attended high school in the 1960s is the generally toxic out-of-classroom culture that erupts during recess (where recess still exists), in the hallways, on school buses, and increasingly now on social media outlets. Study after study demonstrate conclusively that typical middle, junior, and high school life is characterized by rigid hierarchies and social-class divisions, competition for social position, peer dependency, cliques, bullying, rumor-mongering and slander, and racial, ethnic, and linguistic segregation. In other words, schools pretty much mirror the larger society. If anything, schools reflect even deeper levels of exclusion and social cruelty, for adolescents are in the throes of out-of-control hormonal changes, hopeless insecurities, and other intense changes that underpin the Darwinian struggle for identity and social position. When I asked Shaman to reflect upon how he experienced the social world of the middle school when he entered the system, he said without a moment's hesitation, "I was at sea because I didn't understand meanness, bullying, redneckness, crudeness, and groupism." Many might say, "well this is life and they have to learn to deal." But numbers of unschooling families feel otherwise, and in fact have opted out of schools to avoid such negative socialization. And, though the evidence is not all in, most of these kids seem none the worse for missing out on it.

Perhaps I am beginning to sound like one of those overprotective parents who did not want their kids exposed to the harsh realities of life, or who did not think that formal education has anything to offer. Not so. I definitely did not believe that we were the only adults worth learning things from, which is why I helped organize and then took on the directorship of a community-based educational enrichment cooperative. This was at the time, and I suspect still is, a unique response to the inability of the school to provide for the full spectrum of educational needs and interests that our young people have, or which they might have if they were only aware of the possibilities. The Stillwater Cooperative for Educational Enrichment (SCEE) was an informal, affiliated group of mostly university professors and their families who wanted their children exposed to a wider range of skills and knowledge than was provided by the local schools.

Parents in the cooperative offered classes and workshops throughout the year and during school breaks, but things really took off in the summer. I used to joke that our kids experienced most of their formal learning during summer vacation. Seeing as how most of the members were connected to the local university in some way, that vast expanse of resources was at our disposal. Our boys got to learn about the electron microscope from biologists and physicists, dissect grasshoppers with an entomologist, produce and videotape a play with a professional theater director, study plant chromatography with a botanist, observe a Van de Graaf generator in the physics lab, make musical instruments with a luthier, study topological math with a mathematician, take numerous creative-writing workshops with writers, and spend two days reenacting the Battle of Antietam with a historian who had a complete collection of Civil War miniatures on a pool table in his basement.

Membership in the SCEE was not elitist, exclusive, or restricted to university professors. The only criterion for belonging was that you agreed to offer your services to the co-op. When I became the director of it, I aimed for broad community participation. Kids got to learn large-kiln pottery, metal-sculpture casting, and jewelry making with local artists, seine rivers with a fish and wildlife specialist, learn orienteering with an Eagle Scout, and go bird watching with a local member of the Audubon Society. Linking up with other parents, most of whom were not unschoolers, offered an incredible smorgasbord of educational opportunities that we would otherwise not have had access to.

The cooperative offered what the best private schools do: classes in interesting subjects with real experts. (In case you didn't know this, private schools often do not hire state certified teachers. They are free to hire highly knowledgeable people who are passionate about their subjects, and parents pay dearly for this advantage.) Little if no *classroom management* was required, because the content was interesting and kids were there because *they wanted to be.* Because there were no standards to be met, no exit tickets to write (exit tickets are a pedagogical fad that serve to hold students "accountable" for their learning), or tests to be taken at the end of the class, the focus could be on the actual activity and the questions it generated, not on a discrete set of "intended outcomes." I cannot emphasize enough what a difference this makes. When young people are freed from the requirement to learn what someone says they have to learn, rather than what they are interested in, and freed from the necessity to prove that they have learned what others say they are supposed to learn, the resistance that school teachers experience pretty much disappears. The need to coerce kids with reward structures and incentives and to discipline them for noncompliance are all features of a compulsory system of learning. Most kids want to learn and grow and become productive human beings, even if they don't let on at first. All we adults really need to do is to supply the right conditions for this to happen.

SCEE represented what I would call a semi-structured learning environment, somewhere in between formal schooling and unschooling. In such a model, classes are freely available, taught by a wide range of adults who have expertise or a particular passion, and kids take them if they are interested. Learning involves actual activity — no sitting for hours copying notes off a whiteboard or out of a textbook. Classes take place in the real world (in parks and forests, near rivers and lakes, in labs, studios, or people's homes). The consequences are real: if you don't read the compass right, you won't find your destination. If you don't mix the clay right, your sculpture will fall apart. There are no grades, no tests, and no exit tickets. And many kids go on to pursue these activities on their own, after initial exposure.

A model like this balances out the individualism of the unschooler learning primarily on their own with the opportunity to work in a group and develop social learning skills, like questioning, hypothesizing, describing, and co-constructing meaning. No one is forcing kids to use sentence starters, so conversation can be natural, wide ranging, and imaginative, the kind of talk that can result in real discoveries and insights. Kids get to experience a wide range of adults, with all their quirks and unique gifts, not just their daily classroom teacher, and see all the different ways that people approach the natural act of teaching, not just the mechanistic techniques of the trained teacher, like the ubiquitous "Do Now" or the "Turn & Talk" (for one minute) strategy. There are many models out there already for socializing young people to the norms, values, skills, and knowledge of their community. SCEE was my experiment in the 1980s with this, but unschoolers now are leading the way in developing new models and structures.

No one really knows the optimum conditions for socializing young people to become happy and productive adults, to become fully human. The research on school socialization consistently shows that schools have done a pretty poor job at producing kind, tolerant, and engaged citizens. After all, they've been at it for a long time, and if they were models of successful socialization processes, would we be stuck with elected representatives who can't seem to figure out how to negotiate, compromise, get along with others, and work for the common good? Would our crime rate be out of control? Would we in the US have the highest incarceration rate in the world? Would we have a society in which 1% of the population hoards as much of the planet's wealth as they can get hold of?

If the research on school socialization paints a somewhat bleak picture, the research on homeschooling socialization paints a blurry one. Many of the studies fall into the category of "advocacy research" (in which the researcher clearly has a bias towards or against unschooling), or the samples are so small as to not be meaningful. Often the data rely on self-reporting, and there is always a self-selection process involved in this. Rigorous double-blind studies, in which as many potential sources of bias as possible are eliminated, are few and far between. The result is that much of the data about the socialization of unschoolers is anecdotal, including my own. What we do know is that unschooled children do not appear to be turning out to be socially maladjusted in any greater proportion than the schooled population. Unschooled children are generally not prisoners of parents with ultradangerous ideas who are hell bent on brainwashing them. Most unschooled children have a wide range of multigenerational relationships with a variety of people, and most participate in activities outside the home: 4H, sports, church groups, Scouts, etc. Homeschoolers go to college, get jobs, get married (or not), have families, and enjoy leisure time much like other people. Many of them report such positive unschooling experiences that they choose the same route for their own children.

But what, you might be asking, about those left-wing bomb makers and occultists hacking away and blowing up the rural Oklahoma woods? I'm happy to report that they grew up with all their fingers intact and turned into intelligent, competent adults. One is a NASA scientist, one a computer expert at a major university turned entrepreneur, one became a government official in commercial diplomacy, and one a professor of language and religion. All have advanced degrees. All have a wide range of friends and are well connected to their families. Not a Unabomber in the group.

We should probably worry less about the socialization of unschooled children and more about the socialization of an entire generation of young people. In our communities, we should be having serious conversations about why so many young people are turning to drugs for escape and recreation, why social media can be so nasty, why young boys and girls are "sexting," why gay youth are bullied, why suicide is the third leading cause of death among young people ages ten to twenty-four, and why, as Beverly Tatum, a prominent scholar and researcher pointed out, "are all the black kids sitting together in the cafeteria?" When we figure out these sticky issues, we might then turn our attention to the kids whose families are exploring alternative forms of education and socialization.

14 How We Fell From Paradise

Nothing is certain
but that something new will come
infinite turning

~KK

MONEY WASN'T SUPPOSED TO be an issue for our hippie generation. After all, weren't we the avant-garde of the coming anticapitalist, egalitarian society? Seekers of meaning, not seekers of money. Lovers of connection, not lovers of cash. We did have some experience living in a mostly money-free economy in the Huerfano Valley. There, doctors and midwives donated or bartered their services. Poets and musicians and actors performed for free. Farmers shared their crops. But that utopian dream was built upon at least two unsustainable foundations. The first was food stamps, which served as a general, all-around currency. Folks justified taking them as a kind of hoax on the government, allowing the establishment to fund the revolution. Earl and I paid cash or bartered services for everything, however, viewing the food stamp solution as an addiction that would prevent people from ever becoming truly self-sufficient.

The second and far greater problem was the on-going need for hard cash. No matter how much an alternative community reuses and recycles and barters, at some point things need to be imported from the outside world: tractors, tools, medical supplies, appliances. Unfortunately, the solution for a number of Valley dwellers was the production of the most lucrative cash crop in the US (and many other countries): marijuana. When pot was merely a form of community currency, this isolated group of communes was left alone. When sharing turned to selling (to teenagers in Denver), the long eyes of the law turned toward the peaceable kingdom. The Huerfano suffered a predictable dissolution some time after we left when the black helicopters dropped down and busted everyone in sight. A grand experiment in utopian socialism shattered.

Earl and I hung onto our dream of self-sufficiency, perhaps longer than most. But the truth is, we slipped rather precipitously from voluntary simplicity into abject poverty. Things fell apart for us economically in the second half of the 1980s, the result of a fatal combination of factors: a severe recession, the crisis in the savings and loan industry, massive bank failures, and a decline in oil prices. People at all levels of the regional economy were hard hit, but dealers in luxury goods, whose customers were bankers and oilmen, dropped like flies. What did us in was the business model for gem dealers, who put expensive stones on consignment with jewelers who then show them to their high rollers. If a jewelry store goes under, as many of our best customers did during that time, the bank padlocks the doors and seizes everything in the place. We lost most of our inventory that way, many thousands of dollars worth. And gem dealers don't carry insurance. Even Lloyd's of London wouldn't insure a gem dealer (we tried), seeing as men walking into jewelry stores with large suitcases are prime targets for crime.

Other issues conspired with the general economic downturn to bring us to our knees. Some serious physical problems, including the removal of a gall bladder and a fractured leg, put Earl out of commission for weeks at a time. We had no unemployment insurance or workers' comp to draw upon. In fact, we lived without health insurance throughout our entire marriage, raising four boys on a bartering arrangement with a local pediatrician whose wife liked jewelry, and hoping for no serious health crises. The four births had cost us a total of two hundred dollars plus a few colored stones. We felt fortunate indeed when Earl's gall bladder surgeon fancied a pink tourmaline ring from our catalog, but there were still hospital costs.

In hindsight, we were the proverbial canaries in the mineshaft, for it is no longer even news to hear stories about families falling into ruin because of healthcare costs and the loss of employment. It is with grim irony that I listened to my public radio station during the recession of 2008–2009 to hear ordinary middle class citizens saying things like, "We are going to have to change the way we live" and "We're simply going to have to do with less—less fossil fuel, fewer consumer items," etc. Grim, because the potential for genuine cataclysm—some combination of environmental disaster, economic collapse, and social upheaval—no longer seems like the ranting of dissatisfied survivalists, but a real possibility in the not-so-distant future. Irony, because good as it would feel to say "we told you so," any sense of smug self-righteousness is overwhelmed by the fact that our experiment at self-sufficiency fell stunningly short of success. I am in awe of other modern homesteaders who after years of struggle now live on prosperous family farms, run thriving small businesses, and managed to get all of their homeschooled children into Ivy League universities. Our story, though there is much to celebrate in it, is perhaps painfully illustrative of just how hard it is to "unhook" from the system.

The last autumn of our five-year experiment saw me taking a half-time teaching job in an excellent private preschool in town, working with three and four year olds. A university professor encouraged me to enter OSU's graduate program in curriculum and instruction, where I had delivered the occasional lecture on educational alternatives. Steve, once again demonstrating his uncanny ability to adapt to mainstream culture, entered high school. Earl stayed home mornings with the three younger boys while I taught at the preschool. They were mostly on their own as their dad, recovering from illness and injury, tried to keep the business going by phone and stay on top of the paperwork. I'd race home at lunchtime when my morning preschool session was over and try to cram in some learning activities along with the usual household chores. Earl sometimes went out on the road, scrounging up what sales could be found. Steve hung out in the town library doing homework until Earl could pick him up at night. Our relaxed, productive days of unschooling turned into hours spent burning up the gas on the eight-mile dirt road to get me to work, Steve to school, Steve home from school, me to night school, and squeeze in the violin lessons and soccer practice and tai kwan do. Until we couldn't afford those extras anymore.

In spring, the rains turned the dirt road to deep, sticky, red clay. Any vehicle stuck in it simply stayed mired until someone drove by with a strong bumper and a tow chain. In those days before cell phones, if no one drove by, it meant a long hike home. When we were unplugged and off the grid and on our own schedule, we could get snowed in or rained out or broken down and it didn't matter. We would just crank up the woodstove, boil a pot of beans on the fire, and snuggle up with good books by candlelight. But now, we were constantly worried about me missing work or Steve missing school.

Sales were dismal. There was hardly any inventory left in the suitcase after all the jewelry store foreclosures, and the business only limped along because Earl was able to get stones on consignment from a sympathetic dealer in New York. But we could hardly afford the gas to keep driving, and we lived one car repair away from calamity. My salary was barely enough to keep groceries on the table. Earl and I argued. We had never really argued much, perhaps because he was so seldom home. But he was home a lot now and like most other couples with money problems, our stress often blew up into petty squabbles. I was harsh with the kids too, when they did normal kid stuff like bickering with each other when I could see that Earl was hanging by a thin thread. We began bankruptcy proceedings.

One morning, after a particularly grim week, when we were dashing about trying to get everyone organized to drive into the day, I heard a verbal explosion from the kitchen. I had put some ends of bread out for toast. And the kids were wrangling over them. *My children were fighting over crusts of bread!* That day, at the preschool, my red eyes prompted a question or two from my co-teachers. I tried to put up a brave front, to *whistle a happy tune,* but must have let something slip, for when I opened the truck door for my run back to the homestead at noon, there was sixty dollars in cash in an anonymous envelope on the driver's seat. It meant gas and groceries for the week. I never have been a crier; I can count on one hand the times I have truly cried in my adult life. But this simple act of generosity broke the levee.

By summer, given our fraying relationship, the losing battle with the mud roads, and the growing awareness that we were in over our heads, we decided with some regrets but also some relief to find a rental house in town and continue building our dream house. It made a lot of sense. I had been offered a position as an instructor in the College of Education, teaching classes in educational sociology and supervising undergraduate student teachers. It wouldn't pay an enormous amount of money but with the position came tuition remission and scholarships. Sadly, I would have to give up the job I loved at the preschool, but my new position would sort of keep us afloat while Earl figured out what to do next. He had been taking classes in the Political Science master's program at OSU and it looked like he might soon be able to pick up an adjunct course teaching undergrads, thus realizing his pre-Flaming Rainbow dream of being a history teacher. Things were looking up. It was still hectic and we were scrambling for money, but I thought we had a workable plan.

The summer before, I had choreographed *Fiddler on the Roof* for the local *Town and Gown* theater. I had a marvelous time doing it, and the entire family took part in every phase of the production from auditions through rehearsals and set building to the performances. It was one of the best possible unschooling experiences. Shaman helped out backstage. Earl even joined in, playing a priest and a Russian soldier in the pogrom that breaks up Tzeitel's wedding. The show got great reviews and I was reveling in the revival of my show business career, if only in a community theater. When the director asked me this summer to join her team for *Roar of the Greasepaint, Smell of the Crowd*, I eagerly accepted. It would be a bit crazy; we would be looking for a house to rent, I would be taking a full load of graduate credits, and we'd be shuttling all four boys to the usual insane number of Little League baseball games, but we'd manage. Shaman would help build sets for this production and manage the props and he, Chris, and Räm all had small parts.

What I hadn't anticipated was the bombshell Earl dropped.

"Hey, we've got the day free. Let's pick up a paper and see what there is to rent," I said one early summer day.

We'd been to look at a couple of places and so far what we could afford was pretty depressing. Low-rent suburbs, edge of town, cheaply paneled places with smelly, sticky, synthetic carpets. Or worse, a trailer park. We had done that once before, in between houses, and I did not believe my soul could survive such aesthetic trauma again. But I was optimistic that if we kept at it, we'd find something, a place to rest while we finished building our dream house.

"I'm not coming," said Earl, looking away from me.

"W...what do you mean? Do you have something else to do today?"

"Nope. I'm not coming."

"What do you *mean*?"

"I'm not moving with you. You and the boys can get a place in town. I'll stay here."

I could understand his reluctance. Finally, he had a place where he couldn't see the smoke from his neighbor's chimney. I hated to leave too, but it was just temporary.

"We can come out here on weekends, can't we?" I said. "Kind of like camping. But we'll have jobs and enough money to buy materials. We'll probably get it built even faster."

Earl never did talk a lot, but he was uniquely uncommunicative about his intentions in this case. It was a few days before it finally dawned on me that he did not want to be married anymore. At first I didn't believe him. Of course we would work this out. We had been married sixteen years! We had four young kids. I mean, hadn't we fantasized about getting that wrap-around porch built and growing old in our rocking chairs, watching the grasshoppers hop and listening to the toads croak? I slipped back and forth between denial and panic. The more I wanted to talk about it, the deeper within himself he withdrew. There would be no confrontations, no lengthy discussions. I think he just planned to slip quietly out of the relationship, sixties-style. But I was not about to slip quietly out of this marriage. There was too much at stake, primarily the welfare of these four boys of ours. I behaved badly. One night, I threw a very large book at him. It was *Being and Time*. (It missed.) I cried and sulked for a few days. I suggested marriage counseling. I inflicted tremendous guilt on him regarding the likely consequences for the kids. Nothing worked. When Earl made up his mind about something, there was no moving that boulder.

~

Ralph Waldo Emerson famously said, "For everything you have missed, you have gained something else," a secular version of Job's "God gave and God taketh away." I lost a lot that summer—a husband, a planned future, the security of an intact family, my beloved garden, and a dream. But in the uncanny way the universe has of providing you with what you need to heal from your wounds, an extraordinary house fell into my lap through a connection at the theater.

The house on Devon Road was at the edge of town on an isolated cul-de-sac, in the middle of an old pecan grove. It felt like country living but was a block from a paved road and a short bicycle ride from the school that Räm and Chris would attend. Designed and built by an architect, it had elegant red Mexican-tile floors in the living room, huge oak crossbeams, seven sets of French doors, an enormous kitchen, and best of all, a sunken brick-floored solarium, with real dirt around three sides of it. Maybe I couldn't grow vegetables, but my friends filled that room with amazing succulents. The place was magic; more than a house, it was a temple for the reconstruction of my shattered self. The only reason I could afford something like this on my instructor's income and student loans was the fact that fabulous as it looked, the architect's design talents had far exceeded his carpentry skills. Holes where the roof met the siding allowed squirrels to stash their pecans in the attic space, and the more-than-slight slant of the house meant that pecans thus deposited rolled from one end to the other. Often at night we heard those critters playing squirrel soccer up there. Rain dripped through the eaves, rotting the wood siding. The place was slowly sinking into genteel shabbiness, but I absolutely loved it.

So I moved us to town, choreographed *Roar of the Greasepaint, Smell of the Crowd*, took summer courses towards my doctorate, and made sure everybody got to their baseball games, even if I had to sit in the bleachers with my nose buried in textbooks. I enlisted other parents to poke me whenever one of the boys was about to have an at-bat or looked like he might catch a fly ball, so that I could stand up and cheer with the rest of them. I stayed pretty angry for the rest of that summer. I could fathom the fact that Earl would leave *me*, but found it inconceivable that he would abandon the boys. I mean, I probably would have stayed in a truly dismal marriage as long as there were children involved, and while we had certainly hit a rough patch, it didn't seem to be all that bad of a relationship.

What terrified me most was the thought that I might lose custody of the boys, or that they would be separated. But in my heart, I knew Earl wouldn't be able to handle things on his own. He was living out at Camp Paradise, with little furniture and no stove or refrigerator, doing the work of his dreams as a barely paid environmental organizer while applying to a doctoral program in environmental science. No more traveling salesman, a job that he had endured uncomplainingly, but which had never suited his radical soul.

In some ways, the fact that we stayed married for sixteen years during the decades of wife swapping and sexual philandering and communes and open marriage is a testament to something. But whatever we had wasn't strong enough to see us through the multiple crises we faced.

~

Unschooling, or homeschooling, is attachment parenting carried to the nth degree. Long past the infant-bonding stage, unschooling families generally spend a great deal more time together than conventional families. I think it's great when parents figure out ways to divide the responsibilities for this evenly, but we sure never did. I was the homeroom teacher and Earl was the "specials" person. On those occasions when he was home, he taught them to shoot and clean guns, weigh and measure rubies, hammer nails, cast a fishing rod, catch crawdads, pour a foundation, and build a simple electrical circuit. Sometimes he took one or another of them on a road trip. All of which was wonderful, but somewhat rare.

From the beginning, we were right on the same page with the notion of attachment parenting, although we did not have those words for it, and we committed to the whole nine yards—home birth, extended breast feeding, skin-to-skin contact, baby massage, the family bed—and we did it simply because it felt right, not because we were striving to meet any ideal. I'd read Ashley Montague's *Touching: The Human Significance of The Skin* and Joseph Chilton Pearce's *Magical Child*, and we were determined to create an environment of care and connection more akin to that of our primal forbears than to conventional modern child-rearing practices. We rejected such stock features of our own generation's upbringing as high-tech birthing, chemically laced infant formula, canned and processed baby food, and enforced sleeping schedules, which require allowing babies to "cry it out" until they figure out the schedule that the grown-ups want them on. To this day, crying babies break my heart. But with the gendered division of labor that often comes with the territory, attachment parenting too easily becomes attachment mothering. I sometimes worked outside the home (or the tent!), taking the occasional teaching job when I wasn't pregnant or with a new infant, and I did a lot of our office work for the gem business, but Earl was the one with the major responsibility for bringing in the cash, which meant that I got all the pleasure of attachment parenting and he got most of the pain of the money economy. When we separated, there really wasn't much question of who would have responsibility for the kids, and my fears of being separated from them, or having them separated from each other, proved unfounded.

When things fell apart, I failed to comprehend the devastating effect it had on him not to be able to provide for his family anymore. Depression enters the soul in myriad ways. Earl's childhood was an abusive one, with a mother who was the opposite of a nurturing, attached parent. All those whippings he got in school and at home surely left a huge, unhappy hole in his psyche. While I had always celebrated the fact that Earl had not replicated the abuse patterns of his childhood, I just was not aware of the psychic burden that he labored under. He was a strong silent guy after all, and we were busy, and I guess this combined to push away the kind of healing work that we might have done in our marriage, had we the necessary knowledge and skill and perhaps a bit more leisure time. But we had four babies in ten years, and my energy was devoted largely to them, not to the relationship. I guess I took it for granted, figuring it would always be there, like the spring storms or the summer drought. With unschooling, I continued to be absorbed by those mother/child relationships and he was mostly engaged in the struggle for economic survival.

So we fell from Paradise, but we survived the crash. In many ways, we all thrived. Steve outdid himself in high school. It was never necessary to prod him to do his homework, or encourage him to take on challenging academic courses, or to make sure he took the requisite college-entrance exams. In high school, he took two years worth of college courses in chemistry, physics, literature, and philosophy. He was entirely self-directed about all this, and if anything, I worried that he was overdoing it with his all night study sessions and his tendency to take on incredible academic challenges. We have talked about this, and he admits he was worried about "making the grade" when he rejoined the system. He clearly made the grade, and more, but his worries about matching up with his peers does say something about how deeply engrained competitiveness and comparative assessments of self and other are in our culture, even when we attempt to elude them.

Shaman proved a bit of a dilemma to the middle school. When we first visited there to discuss his entry into the sixth grade, the guidance counselor asked him what he was reading. At that point, he was working his way through Homer's classics yet again and trying to learn Greek so he could read them in the original. When he told her this, she said, "Excuse me, I need to go get the principal." The outcome of our visit was that he would skip the sixth grade and go into the seventh. The next year at the Jr. High (which was eighth and ninth grades) he would attend the high school for math and science with the eleventh and twelfth graders in the mornings, and then go back to the Jr. High to socialize with his peers for the rest of the day. This pattern continued until his senior year in Vermont, when he had run out of advanced-placement courses and there were no courses at the local community college that interested him. As a valedictorian for his class, they had to find something for him to do. So he did an independent study in English with a favorite teacher, wrote a term paper on Jungian archetypes, and pursued private studies in violin and classical composition, putting together a portfolio for application to a music conservatory that fall.

It's not at all unusual for home or unschooled children to advance rapidly and dramatically in required school subjects. There are many reasons for this: they are allowed to proceed at their own pace, they can avoid the enormous amount of repetition and redundancy necessary in schools with large classes and uniform curricula, and they are usually engaged in something of their own free will, which eliminates the resistance to learning that students often exhibit. But most important, they have access to a wide range of actual *experiences* and the time to pursue them, which provides a rich context for comprehending more abstract textbook academic learning. Both Shaman and Steve did extremely well in school, though the public school social scene puzzled them at first with its cliques and conflicts and snobberies and petty savageries. But they learned to navigate.

Re-entry was somewhat difficult for Räm and Chris, due to their ages and the fact that neither had ever set foot in a school, other than the preschool where I taught. I took great care in selecting their teachers, whom I briefed ahead of time about our unschooling experiences. This was in the days before the test-prep frenzy hit elementary schools, and the entire staff were enthusiastic proponents of whole language, so the boys had a wonderful exposure to good literature and project-based learning. But at first both of them were overwhelmed by the entire social experience—the playground jungle—and found it disconcerting to have to do things like line up to go places and raise their hands to speak. They were mystified by school routines that other first and third graders had down pat. On their first day of school, everyone disappeared from the cafeteria after the usual lunchtime food fights and shouting and spilt milk. They looked at each other and figured "it must be over" and headed home. Soon, they learned about the big play yard outside one of the cafeteria doors and to join their fellow students for "recess," a concept that I had neglected to teach them. But they made lots of friends and were both very athletic so things very quickly started working out for them in elementary school.

I embarked on single parenting and for my grad-student years worked multiple jobs to keep food on the table. After that first pissed-off summer, I decided that good relations were probably the healthiest approach to splitting up, and Earl and I have remained friends to this day. He continues to be a warrior for the environment, and lives on a four-hundred-acre parcel of land in Oklahoma where he cannot see the smoke from his neighbor's chimney. I finished my doctorate, then moved first to Vermont and then to Brooklyn, then back to Vermont to pursue my career as a writer and professor of curriculum, teaching, and learning.

Though we may have fallen short of bringing about the imminent revolutionary transformation of our consumer society by living a life of ecological sustainability and voluntary simplicity, I do not regret our years in Paradise. The boys had experiences that shaped their lives in many ways. I see how tiny intellectual sparks lit fires that still burn in them. I see them carefully considering the ecological consequences of how they live. I see their thirst for new experiences, for widening their scope of knowing, for reaching out to the world and believing that they can figure anything out if they put their minds to it. And most important, I see them making sensitive and thoughtful decisions about their own children's lives and learning. Truth is, they taught me much of what I know about how children think and how they learn, more than I have gathered from two graduate degrees in education, reading scores of books about the subject, and decades of teaching in formal environments. I shall always be grateful for the opportunity to peer into the possibility of a radically different approach to learning—the notion that we can learn what we need to live happily and successfully in the world with no behavioral objectives, no mandated curricula, no tests, no lessons, no time outs, no motivational techniques, no accountable talk, no grades, no report cards—with no school as we have known it for the last few centuries.

The Next Generation, Vermont 2015

15 So, Do We Need School?

I BEGAN MY JOURNEY INTO unschooling some thirty years ago with the deep conviction that there was a fundamental mismatch between the way children learn and the way schools are designed. While this conviction was affirmed in countless ways, I am now equally convinced that there is a fundamental mismatch between what schools offer and the perils and possibilities of a future hurtling towards us at warp speed.

I suppose the future has always seemed fraught with peril to us fragile Earth dwellers, but because the twenty-first century is one of such tightly woven global interdependence, smaller local disasters have much larger impacts than they might have had in the past. The sheer scale and availability of information means that we are overloaded with news about everything that happens in the world, which plays a part in cultivating a mass psychology of dread. But it's more than a state of mind. The "butterfly effect," the notion from chaos theory that the tiny flapping of a butterfly's wings in a distant location can set off a chain of events that might alter the speed or direction of a tornado, is an apt metaphor for this epoch. Regional banks and economies take a tumble and threaten the global financial structure. Radiation from a disaster at a Japanese nuclear power plant shows up in seaweed on the California coast. Small-scale terrorists in out-of-the-way places have the potential to create and use weapons of mass destruction. I write this closing chapter in the aftermath of Hurricane Sandy, a once-in-a-hundred year storm that walloped my city as well as a third of the country east of the Mississippi. Once-in-a-hundred-year storms have become twice-in-two-years storms here in NYC

one can't help but wonder if the catastrophes that the
ligned environmentalists (us wackos, tree huggers, and
) warned about are upon us. And it's not just climate
change we have to worry about, but the myriad problems related
to a couple centuries worth of poisoning the planet. Those of
us who made our throats raw hollering into the wind about the
dangers of fossil-fuel emissions, soil erosion, ocean pollution,
pesticide-laden foods, loss of species, nuclear power, and a host of
other hazards have actually lived long enough to feel vindicated,
if not celebratory. There is nothing to celebrate about humanity's
swift slide into disaster, an accelerating slide, given our tendency
to choose the health of our GNP over the health and well being
of the Earth.

Meanwhile, the lumbering elephant of a national school system
trundles along, concerned not with questions that matter—*What
do young people need to know to cope with the rapidly changing
world that is upon us? How can we teach our children to live in ways
that protect the biosystems that all life relies on? How can we educate
people for a life of meaning and for work that sustains both themselves
and the planet?*—but with questions of testing and standardization
and accountability. The public conversation about education suffers
from a scandalous disregard for what is truly important and an
appalling lack of imagination. We made the decision to unschool
our children thirty years ago for these very reasons, and there has
been little progress since; in fact, schools have taken a few giant
steps backward since those exuberant "Earth Days" of the 1970s.

In the preface to this book, I spoke about the historical purpose
of school—to *Americanize* the vast number of immigrants in the
late nineteenth and early twentieth centuries, and to indoctrinate
them into the habits and skills necessary for participation in a
rapidly industrializing urban culture. Preparing students for jobs
in our capitalist economy has always been the overriding concern
of our public schools, despite some lip service given to creating
"lifelong learners" and "citizens for a democratic society." The

rhetoric has shifted somewhat now, with references to creating workers who can "compete in the global economy" and live in an "interdependent, diverse world." But the role of schools is clear: to prepare students for participation in a competitive economy, in spite of the fact that we live in a post-industrial society that is changing so rapidly we truly have no idea what jobs will look like five years from now or how to prepare students for them. And surely, the near collapse of the economy in late 2008 and 2009, coupled with continuing instability in the world, might alert us that the economy that schools are supposed to be preparing young people for is precarious at best. I am not advocating a "doom and gloom" curriculum. We need to be very sensitive to the emotional and psychological well being of children and not fill them with a sense of dread and despair about the state of the world. But if kids are not *engaged* in learning, they will not develop the capacities to deal with the problems of the twenty-first century, and in that sense, I believe that most of our current "school reform" initiatives are misguided. I am fond of the metaphor often applied to school reform — that it is a bit like trying to repair the engine of an airplane while in flight. It is a Herculean task to institute significant change while maintaining the necessary stability, so existing structures and practices tend to persist long past their usefulness or relevance. In this sense, schooling is perhaps the most conservative institution in our society.

When we look at the accelerating rate of change in the world alongside the lumbering elephant that we call "school" it is no wonder that so many people have opted to take things into their own hands. The curriculum of the school and the ever-pervasive tests continue to be based on the transmission and regurgitation of ideas in print, more or less disregarding the explosion of the new digital and multimedia-based technologies that saturate the world our young people were born into. While schools struggle to purchase equipment that is outdated a year after they buy it and train thousands of middle-aged teachers how to use SmartBoards, kids are walking around with a universe of information in their pockets and book bags, and many could be training their teachers in social networking, digital storytelling, home-movie production and GarageBand-style composing. Meanwhile, unschoolers are embracing these new technologies: learning languages online, video gaming (playing and producing), meeting up with other unschoolers in their local communities and abroad, and developing a vast multitude of skills watching YouTube instructional videos. Unfettered by existing structures and practices, unschoolers represent a fertile field of educational experimentation, one that we researchers should be paying more attention to.

Despite evidence to the contrary, we still believe that the best way for children to learn is by studying discrete, separate academic disciplines in fifty-minute blocks of time. This in spite of the fact, reported to me by the hundreds of teachers I have worked with in the past quarter century, that many if not most of their students require "external motivation" (candy, points, stickers, pizza parties, grades) to engage with their school work. We know that a key condition for learning is self-driven motivation, a sense of ownership. Who owns the school curriculum? Corporate textbook publishers and test makers. That's who decides what children will learn and when, not kids and families, or even communities anymore. Teachers themselves have relatively little control over what will be learned and when and how. We know that people learn best when information is embedded in a rich and meaningful context, but we still require kids to memorize vast amounts of information for which they have no immediate use. Unschoolers are busy designing—owning—their own lives, putting their knowledge to work taking photographs, making movies, raising animals, writing plays, gardening, traveling, programming computers, cooking, dissecting grasshoppers, going to museums, practicing martial arts, doing science experiments, knitting, or trying to read Homer in Greek. Doing real things, real work, in the real world establishes the conditions for engagement and motivation.

What about that interdependent, diverse world? How good of a job are schools doing preparing children for that? It depends. If we unpack that lofty phrase in the context of educational policy briefs, what it really means is that more and more countries have been integrated, through the proliferation of multinational corporations, into the global capitalist system. And that the successful global professional of the future needs enough cultural competence and second-language skill to negotiate trade deals and consort with their peers in multicultural social settings. In this sense, elite, well-funded schools that require language study and whose families can afford such luxuries as semesters abroad are probably fulfilling this mission. What I do *not* believe it means in these policy briefs, which are generally funded by conservative think tanks and business groups, is what is embodied so beautifully in the preamble of the Earth Charter, a document launched in 2000 at The Peace Palace in The Hague:

We stand at a critical moment in Earth's history, a time when humanity must choose its future. As the world becomes increasingly interdependent and fragile, the future at once holds great peril and great promise. To move forward we must recognize that in the midst of a magnificent diversity of cultures and life forms we are one human family and one Earth community with a common destiny. We must join together to bring forth a sustainable global society founded on respect for nature, universal human rights, economic justice, and a culture of peace. Towards this end, it is imperative that we, the peoples of Earth, declare our responsibility to one another, to the greater community of life, and to future generations.

If we truly value diversity and understand the meanings of "interdependent" and "fragile" we would embrace genuine cultural pluralism, valuing and honoring those histories that are largely absent from the school curriculum, the cultural worldviews that have been cast aside in the interest of economic growth, and the languages that are becoming extinct in the global homogenization that accompanies global integration. Respect for nature and learning to live within its limits would be an essential part of the school curriculum, and young people would be actively engaged in social issues of concern to them: building Habitat for Humanity houses, clearing nature trails, developing community recycling centers, planting community gardens and agro-forests, creating student newspapers, networking with their age peers in other countries, studying conflict resolution and how to build a peaceful world. There is no shortage of good work for young people to be involved in that might help them learn to make the kinds of decisions that could usher in the future envisioned in the Earth Charter.

I agree with philosopher Wendell Berry that the problem is not simply one or another environmental crisis, or gender relations, or even corporate domination of the planet, but a kind of "cultural pathology" that is deeply rooted in our histories, our religion, our national identities, our guiding philosophies, and our education. He envisions a coming "ecozoic era" in which humans overcome our habitual, ruthless exploitation of the Earth, and learn to live in satisfying, self-sustaining, life-enhancing ways. This is a tall order, given that most of the major institutions of our society (economies, political parties, schools) are locked into antiecological mindsets and practices. But I am heartened by the existence of thousands of groups all over the world who have given themselves over to the quest to bring about a more just, humane, and sustainable world. I think perhaps the very decentralized, leaderless movements that are churning up public consciousness and bringing about localized changes—in community-based agriculture, local currencies, housing, participatory grassroots democracy, ethical consumerism—are the heart and soul of how we might bring about larger changes. I see the unschooling movement as a part of that diversified, experimental momentum toward a sustainable future.

Not everyone wants to, or can unschool their kids. We currently have such a dog-eat-dog economy that even in two-parent households, both usually need to work outside the home just to keep the mortgage paid and food on the table. And many households are single-parent households. Many two-parent *and* one-parent families with a strong desire *do* figure out ways to unschool, everything from working at home to cooperative arrangements with other unschoolers. Still, there will be many people who by temperament or lack of interest or resources just don't feel the call. And that's fine! In a diverse world characterized by individual differences, all of these life choices should be honored. So, do we need school?

Yes—and no. We need something. But it is possible that the brick and mortar concept of school, with its restricted ways of organizing space, time, relationships, work, and the flow of information, is an outdated and inadequate template for learning in the twenty-first century. Kids, almost without exception, desire to spend time with their peers. Learning how to negotiate relationships and construct an identity outside the sphere of the family is a crucial part of growing up. A major function of a society should be to marshal its resources for the education and socialization of the next generation. And though self-directed learners can teach themselves many things quite successfully, other things are best learned with the guidance of a teacher or coach: Ballet. Martial Arts. Auto repair. Painting. Brain surgery. We need to think outside the boundaries that have constrained our imaginations, and unschoolers are helping us to do that. They have demonstrated, in addition to self-teaching, that there are all sorts of learning opportunities that are "not-school": apprenticeships, internships, community service, theater groups, learning networks, team sports, and clubs. In an ideal world, unschooling and homeschooling would be two of many existing choices, and whatever larger system we create would be flexible enough to include entry in and out of options, and partial use of options, and the creative use of educational resources. In contrast to conventional trends in education—nation-states moving increasingly towards national curricula with common standards and rigid systems of accountability—I get excited about diversified, decentralized, localized ecosystems of *personalized* educational opportunities. Just as systems of agriculture that mimic natural systems by relying on biodiversity and multiple production systems (incorporating animal husbandry, forestry, and mixed crops, for example), are more resilient in the face of unpredictable change, so a system of schooling that is responsive to local and individual needs and interests may prove more resilient in the face of the enormous changes bearing down upon us.

Some of the best ideas for transitioning beyond conventional ideas about school are old ideas, the products of visionaries who did not live long enough to see their visions actualized. Ivan Illich was a radical thinker, philosopher, priest, and futurist who criticized modern bureaucratic institutions as purveyors of conformity, pollution, mindless consumerism, war, and a host of other social evils. He was the thinker who first coined the phrase "deschooling society," a process that would deinstitutionalize learning and set up in its place webs and networks that would link people who wanted to know something with people who could share their skills or knowledge. His ideas prefigured the Internet, a technological development with unlimited capacity to link up people with common interests and concerns.

James Moffett was a well-respected scholar of English Language Arts whose final book, published right before his death, *The Universal Schoolhouse: Spiritual Awakening Through Education*, sketched the outline of a similar decentralized learning network that would build on what we know about how children learn best. He addresses many of the important questions we need to be asking as we move towards a truly student-centered, community-based paradigm of learning: *How do you provide choice in an ever-expanding universe of educational possibility, and still anchor young people securely so that they have the emotional and social support they need? What structures need to be in place to match up learners with the right resources at the right time? What kind of guidance or counseling should be available for students who have never had the opportunity to be self-directed learners?* Many of his idea are *transitional,* in the sense that if these ideas of choice and freedom and personal growth and sustainability are interesting to us, we need some mechanisms to get from here to there.

The *Foxfire* experiment, upon which much of Flaming Rainbow's philosophy was constructed, involved students back in the 1960s and 70s who embarked with their English teacher upon an ambitious project to collect the stories, interviews, and artifacts from their southern Appalachian community into a series of magazines called *Foxfire.* The magazines were so successful that the students were able to fund a television station in their school, build a museum and heritage center, and do outreach nationally to teachers and students. The good work of the students at this school continues to this day and the *Foxfire* publication has been in continuous production since its inception. Their success is largely attributed to the facts that students themselves chose to create the magazine, the work is grounded in the real life of the community, and the work the students do is not performed for the teacher or for a grade, but for the big, wide world. It is truly work with a purpose: to preserve and celebrate the local culture and their heritage.

Vermont, where I spend part of my time now, has recently legislated that all young people should have the opportunity to develop Personalized Learning Plans and earn all or part of their high school credits engaged in self-directed learning. Two programs that I helped start here sixteen years ago connect young people and their interests up with community mentors. Kids study organic farming, musical production, blacksmithing, theater, interior design, pottery, computer programming, foreign language, or whatever else sparks their passion. It's a bit like unschooling in the context of a public school. These programs have been very successful and now every child in the state will have these opportunities.

The models are out there; we have only to decide, as a society, that we wish to direct human intelligence towards ends that support meaningful human development, creativity, social justice, and the desire to live in mutually beneficial and sustainable ways with the rest of the planet. We must have the vision to prepare young people to imagine and design the tools and practices and systems capable of responding to our rapidly changing circumstances. Creativity is the new currency, say some futurists. And, given the rapid pace of change, the need for learning will be ongoing and continuous over the span of a working lifetime. But this doesn't necessarily mean people will spend their lives in school. On the contrary, the successful people of the future will need to be nimble learners, forging their own paths, self-teaching, learning from peers, and networking in ad hoc groups. Unschoolers provide us with a living laboratory of what is possible, as do those scattered educational alternatives that have not fallen prey to the standards and accountability regime. We should pay attention to these voices and experiments on the margins. They might just be pointing to a future in which most of what we have come to associate with school— lesson plans, required subjects, learning standards, fifty-minute periods, tests, homework, grades, accountable talk, detention, remediation, timeouts, and the Do Now—goes the way of the cane switches and the dunce caps. In their place might emerge a genuine "learning society" in which people individually and collaboratively pursue those things they are passionately interested in, and declare their responsibility to one another, to the greater community of life, and to future generations. If we can think it, we can do it. Anything is possible.

Acknowledgements

Unschooling in Paradise has been a long time in the making. Originally conceived as a series of essays on children and learning grounded in the narratives from the five years we "unschooled" in the 1980's, the book took a marked turn towards memoir when I joined a writer's group in Manhattan in 2011. I suppose it was unrealistic to think that the sophisticated women in that group – Elizabeth Bailey, Gail Krausner, Lindsey Anthony, and my best writing buddy ever, Monica Rose – could easily grasp why a seemingly cultured, highly educated professor at a large urban university could once have chosen to live in a remote wilderness area with her husband and four children, gone off-the-grid big time, and engaged in this radical thing they had never heard of – unschooling. They simply could not connect the dots between who I was in the present and the story I told about the experiment we had undertaken back then. They insisted I provide them with "backstory," and so the book evolved in ways I could not have foreseen. I hope it is stronger as a result.

I thank my many colleagues and co-presenters in the curriculum field for their kind attention to these radical ideas and helpful feedback at annual conferences: the American Association for the Advancement of Curriculum Studies and the American Educational Research Association, specifically the Ivan Illich Special Interest Group. I appreciated the opportunity to read a part of the Prologue at the San Miguel Writers Conference. And special thanks go to the academic journals that published early versions of some of these chapters: "Doing Good Science: On the Virtues of Simply Messing About" appeared in both *Encounter: Education for*

Meaning and Social Justice and in *Paths of Learning*; "Tarantulas in the Freezer" appeared in the *Trumpeter: Journal of Ecosophy*; and parts of different chapters were woven into an essay, "Unschooling, Then and Now," (with Kellie Rolstad) in the *Journal of Unschooling and Alternative Learning*.

Many thanks to Donald Acosta, for his careful editing, and his willingness to take on this somewhat hybrid project that blurs the lines between essay, memoir, narrative non-fiction, and manifesto!

Mostly I must thank my family – especially my four "boys" (all middle-aged men now!), their wives Kine, Ayesha, and Alexa, my three precious granddaughters Anika, Revati, and Freya, and of course Earl. They have sat patiently through various holiday readings, answered innumerable questions that mostly began with "Do you remember when…?, corrected me when my memory erred, and have been tremendously good sports about this whole project.

About the author

Kathleen Kesson is a tenured Professor of Teaching, Learning and Leadership in the School of Education at LIU-Brooklyn, where she teaches courses in the foundations of education and teacher inquiry. Prior to her scholarly career, she was a professional dancer, actor, choreographer, teacher, and community activist. Her work appears in numerous academic journals and in the books *Curriculum Wisdom: Educational Decisions in Democratic Societies* and *Understanding Democratic Curriculum Leadership* (both with James Henderson) and *Defending Public Schools: Teaching for a Democratic Society* (with Wayne Ross). She divides her time between Brooklyn, New York, and Barre, Vermont, where she is deeply involved in research on personalized learning in Vermont schools.